RESEARCH WRITING IN EDUCATION AND PSYCHOLOGY

ABOUT THE AUTHOR

Eminent professor and caring mentor, productive researcher and author, and creative developer of theory, Herbert J. Klausmeier focused his professional career on improving classroom learning through research. His peers recognize him as an inspirational leader in research in education and psychology.

Herbert J. Klausmeier is the V.A.C. Henmon Emeritus Professor, Unversity of Wisconsin, Madison. He was awarded a B.S. degree in 1940 and an M.S. degree in 1947 by Indiana State University; an Ed.D. degree by Stanford University in 1949. After receiving the Ed.D., he was on the faculty of Northern Colorado University, 1949-1952; the University of Wisconsin, Madison, 1952-1986; the University of Hawaii, summer 1962; and the University of California, Berkeley, summer 1965. He served as the major advisor of many Ph.D. and M.S. degree recipients. He is author or coauthor of 12 books that report empirical research and theory, 33 chapters of edited books, 200 journal articles and technical reports, and 5 college textbooks–3 in multiple editions and 2 translated in several languages.

Professor Klausmeier's peers have honored him by electing him President of the Rocky Mountain Branch of the American Psychological Association, 1951-1952, and President of Division 15, Educational Psychology, of APA, 1970-1971. Other recognitions are the Alumni Distinguished Service Award given by Indiana State University in 1962, the V.A.C. Henmon Professorship by the University of Wisconsin in 1968, the Award for Outstanding Contributions to Education Through Research by Phi Delta Kappa in 1985, and the Edward Lee Thorndike Award for Distinguished Psychological Contribution to Education by Division 15 of APA in 1991. He became a Fellow in APA in 1958 and in 1999 a charter member of the National Academy for Educational Research. His biography is included in *2000 Outstanding Scientists of the 20th Century, Who's Who in America,* and *Who's Who in the World.*

RESEARCH WRITING IN EDUCATION AND PSYCHOLOGY– FROM PLANNING TO PUBLICATION

A Practical Handbook

By

HERBERT J. KLAUSMEIER, Ed.D.

V.A.C. Henmon Professor Emeritus
University of Wisconsin, Madison

Senior Research Consultant
Academic Information Center

LB
2369
.K54
2001
West

Charles C Thomas
P U B L I S H E R • L T D.
SPRINGFIELD • ILLINOIS • U.S.A.

Published and Distributed Throughout the World by

CHARLES C THOMAS • PUBLISHER, LTD.
2600 South First Street
Springfield, Illinois 62794-9265

This book is protected by copyright. No part of
it may be reproduced in any manner without
written permission from the publisher.

©2001 by CHARLES C THOMAS • PUBLISHER, LTD.

ISBN 0-398-07156-X (hard)
ISBN 0-398-07157-8 (paper)

Library of Congress Catalog Card Number: 00-053650

With THOMAS BOOKS *careful attention is given to all details of man-
ufacturing and design. It is the Publisher's desire to present books that are satisfactory as to their physical qualities and artistic possibilities and appropriate for their particular use.* THOMAS BOOKS *will be true to those laws
of quality that assure a good name and good will.*

Printed in the United States of America
CR-R-3

Library of Congress Cataloging-in-Publication Data

Klausmeier, Herbert J. (Herbert John), 1915-
    Research writing in education and psychology--from planning to
publication : a practical handbook / by Herbert J. Klausmeier.
        p. cm.
    Includes bibliographical references and index.
    ISBN 0-398-07156-X (hard) -- ISBN 0-398-07157-8 (pbk.)
    1. Report writing--Handbooks, manuals, etc. 2. Education--
Authorship--Handbooks, manuals, etc. 3. Psychology--Authorship--
Handbooks, manuals, etc. I. Title.

LB2369 .K54 2001
808'.06615--dc21

                                                    00-053650

PROLOGUE

Research Writing in Education and Psychology—From Planning to Publication: A Practical Handbook presents guidelines that cover the entire writing and publication process, from planning to write up a study through reading typeset proofs and transmitting to a journal editor. The *Handbook* is for graduate students, faculty members, and practitioners when preparing manuscripts for journal publication. Instructors may use it as a primary textbook in courses and workshops that focus on conducting and reporting research and as a supplementary textbook in methods courses.

This Prologue gives suggestions for using the *Handbook* and for getting supplementary material and expert assistance if needed. When used effectively, the *Handbook* may provide all the information that manuscript authors need to write a manuscript. However, there are times when a writer may require supplementary material, for example, an issue of a journal to get the instructions about editorial style or a dictionary to find the abbreviation of a technical term. Moreover, a difficult problem occasionally arises, for example, when a manuscript is rejected. Expert assistance may be necessary for revising the manuscript and getting it accepted for publication.

Using the Handbook

Not all of the *Handbook* content is to be used in the same way. Also, researchers and administrative assistants who prepare manuscripts for researchers will use it differently. Getting an overview of the *Handbook* contents will facilitate learning to use it effectively.

Chapter 1, Introduction, indicates preliminary steps that maximize the prospects for getting a study written up and published: weighing the benefits of publication, attending to ethical principles, evaluating the quality of a study, ascertaining differences in the acceptance rates of journals, assessing competence in research writing, and capitalizing on the motive to achieve success.

Chapter 2, Developing a Plan for Writing a Research Manuscript, offers suggestions for developing a time schedule and for arranging a physical environment conductive to writing. Also discussed are selecting a journal, generating an outline, and being brief and concise so as to meet the selected journal's requirement regarding the length of manuscripts.

Chapter 3, Writing Style, Grammar, and Bias in Language, focuses on expository writing style, giving particular attention to developing unified paragraphs that present ideas concisely, precisely, and logically. The chapter also supplies rules of grammar with examples and indicates how to avoid biased language related to sexual orientation, race and ethnicity, disabilities, gender, and aging.

Chapters 4, 5, and 6 present material that conforms to editorial styles in general, including the style given in the *Publication Manual of the American Psychological Association* (American Psychological Association, 1994). However, the guidelines in Chapter 7 are for adhering to the *Publication Manual of APA* only. The titles for these chapters follow:

Chapter 4, Punctuation, Capitalization, Spelling, Hyphenation, Italics, Abbreviations, and Seriation;

Chapter 5, Numbers, Metric Measurement, Statistical and Mathematical Material, Headings, and Quotations;

Chapter 6, Footnotes, Notes, Tables, and Figures; and

Chapter 7, Reference Citations in the Text and References in the Reference List.

Chapter 8, Submitting a Manuscript and Responding to Editorial Review, gives guidelines for preparing a manuscript, submitting it, and responding successfully to editorial review when a manuscript is accepted conditional on revision or when it is rejected.

Appendix A, Citations in the Text and in the Reference List That Conform to *The 1993 Chicago Manual of Style*, provides guides and examples of this editorial style.

Appendix B, Journals in Psychology and in Education Grouped According to Content and Rejection Rates, presents the rejection rates for groups of journals that have similar content and that are published in the English language in the United States and other countries.

Appendix C, Manuscript Submission Letter, Editors' Evaluations of Submitted Manuscripts, and Evaluation Forms for Manuscript Reviewers, provides samples of these materials.

Appendix D, Formats for Electronic References Recommended by the American Psychological Association (1999, November 19), gives the formats that supersede the style for electronic references given in the 1994 *Publication Manual of APA.*

Researchers profit from studying Chapters 1, 2, and 8 before starting to write a manuscript. Only an overview of Chapters 3-7 and the Appendixes suffices before starting to write. Later, any specific information can be located.

Administrative assistants need an overview of the Contents and the Index. These aids will enable them to locate any information they may require when preparing a manuscript for a researcher.

Regarding editorial style, whether Chapter 7 or Appendix A will be relevant depends on the style adopted by the journal to which a manuscript will be submitted. Chapter 7 shows how to cite references in the text and in the reference list to meet the editorial style given in the 1994 *Publication Manual of APA.* The material in Appendix A indicates how to adhere to the editorial style of *The Chicago Manual of Style* (University of Chicago Press, 1993).

Other aids for using the *Handbook* merit a brief note. Examples are set apart from the guidelines to make their identification easy. Also, there are tables and exhibits that supply large amounts of detailed information, such as statistical abbreviations and abbreviations for the 50 states and the territories.

Getting Supplementary Information on Writing Style and Editorial Style if Needed

This *Handbook* supplies information on writing style and editorial style needed for writing typical empirical studies, literature reviews, and theoretical articles. However, supplementary resources that may be helpful in some situations are listed throughout the book and in the Readings. A few of these merit immediate attention.

Relative to writing style, the *New Oxford Guide to Writing* (Kane, 1994) supplies instructions for developing coherent paragraphs and composing clear, effective sentences. *Words Into Type* (Warren, 1992) gives comprehensive information on grammar and on the use of words. Both of these books are addressed to the scholarly community. *Write Right* (Furnish, 1996) and *The Elements of Style* (Strunk & White, 1999) are addressed to an audience whose knowledge of terms, such as *subjunctive mood* or *dangling prepositional modifiers,* needs updating in order to apply rules of grammar. *Roget's International Thesaurus* (Chapman, 1996) is helpful for selecting words that convey the intended meaning.

Merriam-Webster's Collegiate Dictionary (1998) is updated annually. In addition to the usual content of dictionaries, it features the most recent terminology on electronic media. It has useful tables and lists. To illustrate, one table presents metric measurements and another one provides proofreaders' marks. The lists include one on mathematical signs and symbols. *Webster's Third New International Dictionary* (1993) has additional tables and lists. The editorial style for the material in the tables and lists in both dictionaries is the same as that in this *Handbook* and the *Publication Manual of APA.*

Material is becoming available electronically for aiding researchers with all aspects of research writing, for example:

Writing style and grammar: *The Elements of Style* (Strunk, 1999).

Editorial style: *Electronic Reference Formats Recommended by the American Psychological Association* (American Psychological Association, 1999, November 19).

Content of journals: APA journals (http://www.apa.org/journals/homepage.html); *Psychological Abstracts* (http://www.apa.org/psycinfo/products/psycabs.html).

Research writing in general for new writers: *APA Style Helper 2.0: Software for New Writers in the Behavioral Sciences* (http://www.apa.org/apastyle/).

The World Wide Web addresses for the first two electronic documents are given in the reference list of this *Handbook*. It should be noted that locating a particular item in an electronic document usually takes considerably more time than in a printed publication. For this reason, the above document on editorial style is reproduced in Appendix D of this *Handbook*.

Securing Expert Assistance if Beneficial

A writer may experience difficulty in composing a well organized manuscript or in developing unified paragraphs and clear, concise sentences that include the best choice of words. Difficulty may be encountered in presenting the method clearly and concisely, expressing the results accurately, and in relating the problem, method, and results coherently and logically. Of equal or greater importance, a writer may not be able to respond successfully to a negative evaluation received from a journal editor. Chapters 2, 3, and 8 of the *Handbook* along with other supplementary information may be insufficient for dealing with these difficulties. Even if sufficient, expert assistance may save a writer many hours of time and eliminate much stress.

Assistance may be obtained in a number of ways. One source is a colleague, the chairperson of a dissertation committee, the advisor, or the major professor. Help may also be obtained by making an informal oral presentation to students or colleagues. Another possibility is a poster session, symposium contribution, or paper at a meeting of a professional organization. When making an informal or a formal report, invite questions and comments. Try to get constructive criticism that will contribute to producing a high-quality manuscript.

Assistance may come from individuals and groups who offer confidential consultation directed solely to aiding researchers get their studies published. The consultation services are advertised in publications of professional organizations such as the *APA Monitor*. Some services are available on line.

A third kind of assistance in getting research published is provided by professional organizations. Both the American Educational Research Association and the American Psychological Association at their annual conventions provide mentoring, courses, and pre- and postsessions especially for researchers who have little or no publication experience. The offerings are featured in the printed program distributed to association members in advance of the annual meeting. To illustrate, the program for the 2000 annual meeting of AERA listed pre- and postsessions of two days and also of one and one-half days, four-hour minicourses during the annual meeting, and extended courses running for a full day on the first day of the meeting. Participation was encouraged. In fact, the American Educational Research Association (1999) announced ten stipends in the amount of $300 each to support the participation of minority doctoral candidates in a full-day course, "Demystifying the Research and Writing Process for Underrepresented Scholars."

The practical nature of this *Handbook* should now be apparent. It provides the information a writer may need about writing style, grammar, bias in language, and the editorial style of either the *Publication Manual of APA* or *The Chicago Manual of Style*. Moreover, it does not present the many pages of material in these manuals that is primarily for journal editors and production personnel but not for manuscript authors. In addition, this *Handbook* presents much practical information that is not included in either of the preceding manuals or in any given specialized manual: guidelines for preparing to write a manuscript, suggestions for responding to editorial review of a manuscript, a list of journals grouped according to content and rejection rate, sample manuscript submission letters and editors' evaluations of manuscripts, the most recent style of the American Psychological Association for citing electronic documents, and Internet addresses for important electronic documents. Having this practical *Handbook* at one's computer will eliminate the need for having others.

CONTENTS

Page

Prologue v

Chapter

1. INTRODUCTION 3
Weighing Benefits From Getting Research Published 3
Attending to Ethical Principles 3
Evaluating the Quality of a Study 5
Ascertaining Differences Among Journals in Rejection Rates 6
Evaluating Competence in Conforming to Style Requirements 6
Capitalizing on the Motive to Achieve Success 7

2. DEVELOPING A PLAN FOR WRITING A RESEARCH MANUSCRIPT 8
Developing a Time Schedule 8
Arranging a Physical Environment Conducive for Writing 8
Selecting a Journal 9
Preparing an Outline 12
Planning to Meet Manuscript Length Requirements 12
   Preparing More Than One Manuscript 12
   Favoring Brevity and Conciseness 13
      Narrow the problem area 13
      State the problem concisely 13
      Make the literature review brief 13
      Include only the essentials of the method 13
      Be selective in presenting and discussing the results 14

3. WRITING STYLE, GRAMMAR, AND BIAS IN LANGUAGE . . 15
Writing Style 15
   Sequence the Parts of a Manuscript Logically 15

Develop Unified Paragraphs 16
Develop Sentences That Express Ideas Concisely, Precisely,
and Logically 18
Grammar 22
Nouns 22
Pronouns 22
Verbs and Verbal Phrases 24
Adjectives and Adverbs 26
Prepositions and Prepositional Phrases 27
Conjunctions 28
Express Ideas in Parallel Form 29
Bias in Language 30
Avoid Bias Related to Sexual Orientation 31
Avoid Bias Related to Race and Ethnicity 32
Avoid Bias Related to Disabilities 33
Avoid Bias Related to Gender 34
Avoid Bias Related to Aging 35

4. PUNCTUATION, CAPITALIZATION,
SPELLING, HYPHENATION, ITALICS, ABBREVIATIONS,
AND SERIATION 37
Punctuation 37
Period and Question Mark 37
Colon 38
Semicolon 38
Comma 39
Dash 40
Parentheses 41
Brackets 42
Quotation Marks 43
Apostrophe 44
Ellipsis Points 45
Slash 45
Capitalization 45
Spelling 47
Hyphenation 48

Italics 49
Abbreviations 50
Seriation 52

5. NUMBERS, METRIC MEASUREMENT, STATISTICAL
   AND MATHEMATICAL MATERIAL, HEADINGS, AND
   QUOTATIONS 53
   Numbers 53
      Use Figures 53
      Use Words 54
      Use a Combination of Figures and Words to Express Rounded
         Large Numbers and Back-To-Back Modifiers 55
      Place a Comma Between Groups of Three Digits in Large
         Numbers 55
      Exceptions for Comma Usage 55
      Add *s* or *es* Without an Apostrophe to Form the Plural of
         Figures and Words Representing Numbers 55
      Use Figures and Words to Represent Ordinal Numbers in
         the Same Way as Cardinal Numbers 55
   Metric Measurement 55
   Statistical and Mathematical Material 56
      Use Symbols and Abbreviations When Reporting Statistical
         Material 56
      Use Symbols and Abbreviations When Presenting
         Mathematical Equations 59
   Headings 59
      Example 1. Research Report With Headings of Two Levels . . 60
      Example 2. Research Report With Headings of Three Levels . 61
      Example 3. Research Report With Headings of Four Levels . . 62
   Quotations 63
      Reproducing Quoted Material 63
      Crediting Sources and Securing Permission 64

6. FOOTNOTES, NOTES, TABLES, AND FIGURES 65
   Footnotes and Notes 65
      Footnotes 65
      Author Note 65
      Numbering and Submitting Footnotes and Notes 66

Tables 67
   Title 67
   Headings 67
   Table Ruling 67
   Table Notes 68
   Citing and Numbering Tables 68
   Explaining Table Information in the Text 68
   Submitting Tables 68
Figures 69
   Graphs 69
   Charts 70
   Drawings 70
   Photographs 71
   Figure Captions and Legends 71
   Size and Proportion of Figures 71
   Citing and Numbering Figures 72
   Handling Completed Figures 72
   Submitting Figures and Captions 72

7. REFERENCE CITATIONS IN THE TEXT AND
   REFERENCES IN THE REFERENCE LIST 73
  Reference Citations in the Text 73
   One Author 73
   Two Authors 74
   Three, Four, or Five Authors 74
   Six or More Authors 74
   Groups as Authors 75
   No Author 75
   Anonymous Work 75
   Two Authors With the Same Surname 75
   Two or More Publications by Different Authors 76
   Two or More Publications by the Same Author(s) Having
      the Same Publication Date 76
   Two or More Publications in Different Years by the Same
      Authors 76
   Parts of a Source 76
   Personal Communications 76

References in the Reference List 77
  Abbreviation of Terms 77
  Location of Publishers 77
  Articles in Journals, Magazines, Newsletters, Newspapers,
    Special Issues of Journals, and Journals Published
    Annually 79
  Monographs and Abstracts 82
  Books, Booklets, Manuals, and Book Supplements–
    Varying Authorship 83
  Books, Book Articles, and Book Chapters–Varying Editorship . 85
  Research and Technical Reports 86
  Papers and Symposium Contributions 87
  Manuscripts 88
  Reviews 89
  Published Tests 89
  Audiovisual Media 89
  Doctoral Dissertations and Theses 90
  Electronic Media 91
  Statutes, Legislative Materials, Court Decisions, and
    Executive Orders 92
  Sample Reference List 94

8. SUBMITTING A MANUSCRIPT AND RESPONDING
   TO EDITORIAL REVIEW 97
   Preparing and Submitting a Manuscript 97
     Word Processing a Manuscript 97
       Title page 98
       Abstract 98
       Page numbering and manuscript page headers 99
       Order of text and other pages 99
       Copies 100
     Cover Letter to Journal Editor 100
   Responding to Editorial Review 100
     Revising a Manuscript Accepted Conditional on Revision . . . 100
     Options for Publication of a Rejected Manuscript 101
     Securing Expert Assistance 102

Manuscript Review and Proofreading 102
   Reviewing the Copyedited Manuscript 103
   Reading the Typeset Proof 103
After Publication of the Article 103
Author Responsibilities 104
REFERENCES 105

READINGS 107

APPENDIX A. REFERENCE CITATIONS IN THE TEXT AND
REFERENCES IN THE REFERENCE LIST THAT CONFORM
TO THE 1993 *CHICAGO MANUAL OF STYLE* 108
Contents 108
Reference Citations in the Text 111
   Basic Form of Citations 111
   Three Ways to Enter Text Citations 113
References in the Reference List 114
   Books 114
   Parts of a Book 116
   Editions, Multivolumes, Editors, and Series 117
   Periodicals 117
   Reviews in Periodicals 118
   Personal Communications 119
   Unpublished Material 119
   Special Types of References 120
Public Documents 120
   Hearings 120
   Laws, Public Acts, and Statutes 120
   Executive Department Documents 121
   Federal Court Decisions 122
   International Bodies 122
Nonbook Materials 123
Computer Software and Electronic Documents 124
   Computer Software 124
   Electronic Documents 125
Sample Reference List 125

APPENDIX B. JOURNALS IN PSYCHOLOGY AND IN
EDUCATION GROUPED ACCORDING TO CONTENT
AND REJECTION RATES 128

APPENDIX C. MANUSCRIPT SUBMISSION LETTER,
EDITORS' EVALUATIONS OF SUBMITTED MANUSCRIPTS,
AND EVALUATION FORMS FOR MANUSCRIPT
REVIEWERS 131

APPENDIX D. FORMATS FOR ELECTRONIC REFERENCES
RECOMMENDED BY THE AMERICAN PSYCHOLOGICAL
ASSOCIATION (1999, NOVEMBER 19) 138

INDEX: CHAPTERS 1–8 ....

INDEX: APPENDIX A ....

ABOUT THE AUTHOR ....

TABLES AND EXHIBITS

Table 5.1. Frequently used statistical abbreviations and symbols 57
Exhibit 6.1. Example of an author note 66
Exhibit 7.1. Abbreviations in nonlegal references, in legal references,
and for the states and territories 78
Exhibit 7.2. Sample reference list that conforms to the editorial style
of the *Publication Manual of the American Psychological
Association* 95
Exhibit A1. Sample reference list that conforms to the editorial style
of *The Chicago Manual of Style* 126

RESEARCH WRITING IN EDUCATION
AND PSYCHOLOGY

Chapter 1

INTRODUCTION

Taking some proven preliminary steps before starting to write a research manuscript maximizes the prospects for getting a study published. Carefully weighing the benefits of publication, attending to the ethical principles that underlie research writing, and evaluating the quality of a study are essential. Ascertaining differences in the rejection rates of journals, recognizing the competence required to meet the style requirements of journals, and capitalizing on the motive to achieve success also increase the prospects for publication.

Weighing Benefits From Getting Research Published

The extrinsic rewards to the individual from getting research published include obtaining a desired position, advancing in a position, and getting a raise in salary. The publish-or-perish concept is well understood by the research community. Less well known are the intrinsic rewards to the individual and the benefits that accrue to society.

Many researchers experience satisfaction from knowing that they have increased knowledge in their field and that professors and graduate students in major universities worldwide have access to the new ideas. They also appreciate the fact that policy makers and practitioners are increasingly turning to research for guidance. Examining a few issues of the *APA Monitor* gives a good picture of research influencing governmental policy related to improving child care, reducing violent crime, extending psychological therapy, and improving other critical aspects of daily life.

Attending to Ethical Principles

Ethical conduct in research writing entails reliability and honesty (American Psychological Association, 1992a, 1994; Canter, Bennett, Jones, &

Nagy, 1994; Nagy, 1999). The principles that follow apply to the entire writing and publication process:

- The manuscript contains only data that have not been reported elsewhere.
- Permission is obtained to reproduce copyrighted material.
- Credit is given for material that is paraphrased.
- Data are not fabricated and the results are drawn reliably and reported accurately.
- Authors send the journal a correction if they find an error after a manuscript has been published.
- Authors store the study data for at least five years so that interested people can access it.

Ethical conduct pertaining to authorship merits special attention. Authorship is for those who are responsible for the conduct of the study and the interpretation of the results (Fine & Kurdek, 1993). Anyone who has written part of the manuscript or has made some other important contribution, for example, in reviewing the literature or interpreting the results, is included as an author. The name of the principal contributor comes first; others appear in the order of the importance of their contributions. Those who have contributed in a significant but minor way are recognized in a note.

Reaching agreement on authorship should take place before any writing of a manuscript begins as may be illustrated in connection with manuscripts based on dissertations. If the chairperson of the dissertation committee does not make an important contribution to the substance of the study and will not participate in writing the manuscript, the dissertation author should be the sole author. However, a chairperson may make an important contribution and may also desire to be a coauthor. In this case, the dissertation author should be the first author and the chairperson the second.

Situations often develop where agreement on authorship is not reached. For example, a dissertation author refuses to write a manuscript. However, the research must be reported to meet the requirements of the agency funding the chairperson's research program–no published article, no further funding of the program that is also supporting other Ph.D. candidates. Not writing the manuscript borders on being unethical. In another setting, the chairperson, after editing a manuscript written by the dissertation author, puts the chairperson's name first on a manuscript and submits it to a journal. This behavior is unethical. Problems such as these are usually referred to a university official or a committee responsible for graduate studies.

Evaluating the Quality of a Study

Does a study merit publication? A most important consideration is the quality of the content. In general, journals that publish research in education, psychology, and related fields have adopted the following criteria for evaluating empirical studies:

- The research question is important.
- The literature reviewed is relevant.
- The hypotheses are clear and comprehensible.
- The research design permits the hypotheses to be tested.
- The participants are representative of the population to whom the results apply.
- The reliability and validity of the data gathering devices are satisfactory.
- The procedure for gathering the data is sound.
- The statistical analyses are appropriate.
- The results are clear and meaningful.

While gathering data for their studies, researchers typically think their study meets the criteria. Nevertheless, a thorough evaluation of the study is in order before beginning to write a manuscript so that if a problem is found it can be remedied early.

A weakness in a study (for example, in the review of the literature, the data analysis, or the results) is difficult for a researcher to identify independently. However, resources are available to help researchers evaluate their studies and eliminate any deficiencies they may find.

Meltzoff (1998) wrote a book designed to develop competence in the analysis of research reports. He first explained kinds of research. Then he described exemplary practices and pointed out flaws in research articles, starting with the research problem and concluding with the data analysis and discussion. In the second half of the book, he presented many articles that have flaws and gave enlightening critiques that identified the problems. The critiques imply ways to eliminate the flaws and produce an acceptable manuscript.

Wiersma (2000) has a chapter on the correct use of research designs, including experimental, quasi-experimental, survey, qualitative, historical, and ethnographic. Study of the relevant chapter will aid in identifying a flaw in the design of a study and also possible means of eliminating it.

Expert assistance with the evaluation of a study often proves helpful. One means of getting help is to make an oral presentation to peers and get their comments. Another possibility is to discuss the study with a researcher who has experience as a manuscript reviewer. Members of dissertation committees and administrators who help professors get funding to support their research have experience in evaluation. It is important to recognize that assistance in evaluating and improving a study is quite readily available.

Ascertaining Differences Among Journals in Rejection Rates

Chapter 2 deals with preparing to write a manuscript, including the selection of the journal to which to submit a manuscript. The discussion here is concerned only with a frequently overlooked matter–differences among journals in the rejection of manuscripts.

Some journals submit manuscripts to stringent review. They receive more manuscripts than they can accept because they are limited in the number of pages they can print yearly. These journals have high rejection rates. Other journals also review the manuscripts received and have a firm page allocation; however, they receive fewer manuscripts and have moderate rejection rates. A feature of the preceding journals is that they do not charge authors for publishing their manuscripts. Other journals have relatively low rejection rates. Some of them have per-page or other charges and flexible page arrangements. The manuscripts received may not be reviewed except by the journal editor.

An article in a journal with a higher rejection rate may present no more important subject matter than one in a journal with a lower rate. Accordingly, a survey of journals that cover the type of subject matter of a study but that have different rejection rates is in order. This is the first step in selecting a journal to which to submit a manuscript.

Evaluating Competence in Conforming to Style Requirements

Competence in writing in an expository style, using standard grammar, is required for research writing. Also, bias in language related to sexual orientation, race and ethnicity, disabilities, gender, and aging must be avoided. Chapter 3 gives guidelines regarding these topics.

Competence in adhering to editorial style is also demanded of manuscript writers. Editorial style deals with rules regarding mechanical details, including punctuation and spelling, reporting statistical and mathematical material, preparing tables and figures, and citing references in the text and in the reference list. Journals in psychology, education, and related fields use the editorial style spelled out in the *Publication Manual of APA* (American Psychological Association, 1994) or *The Chicago Manual of Style* (University of Chicago Press, 1993). Chapters 4-7 of this *Handbook* give rules and examples in accord with the *Publication Manual of APA* and Appendix A does the same for *The Chicago Manual of Style*.

Although both expository writing and editorial style are demanding, conforming to them does not require exceptional writing competence. Anyone who has completed a graduate program has the competence required for meeting the demands; no further evaluation is necessary. In fact, quite a few manuscripts are written by undergraduates and are published in prestigious journals.

Capitalizing on the Motive to Achieve Success

The motive to achieve success and the corollary motive to avoid failure is present in all of us. These motives exert a powerful influence on daily activities as well as on long-term accomplishments. For example, one individual who feels that there is a 50/50 chance that a manuscript will be accepted starts to prepare the manuscript and persists until it is completed. This action follows from the motive to achieve success. Another individual also surmises that there is a 50/50 chance of manuscript acceptance. This individual does not prepare the manuscript. The inactivity of this individual stems from the motive to avoid failure.

The motive to avoid failure and the resultant turning away from writing a manuscript can be changed through acquiring reliable information. Anyone who has completed a high-quality study should realize that a manuscript based on it will be accepted for publication, provided that the journal to which the manuscript is sent is selected appropriately. Of course, the manuscript must meet the journal's style requirements. As was indicated earlier, this is not particularly difficult.

The importance of getting a first manuscript published is reflected in the careers of many Ph.D. recipients. Some of them prepared a manuscript and sent it to a journal that had a high rejection rate. The manuscript was rejected and this rejection ended research writing for them. The motivation to avoid failure was overwhelming and their careers were affected negatively. Other Ph.D. recipients reworked the rejected manuscript, sent it to a suitable journal, and it was published. When this occurred, continuing to conduct research contributed markedly to advancing their careers.

Chapter 2

DEVELOPING A PLAN FOR WRITING A RESEARCH MANUSCRIPT

Preparing to write a manuscript involves developing a time schedule for writing and arranging a physical environment conducive to writing. Selecting a journal that covers the subject matter of the study and that has a suitable acceptance rate is essential. Preparing an outline of the manuscript saves subsequent writing time and contributes to a clearly organized, concisely written manuscript. Meeting a journal's requirement regarding manuscript length is difficult. The last section of this chapter gives suggestions for preparing to write an appropriately brief, concise manuscript.

Developing a Time Schedule

Preparing a manuscript requires time. It cannot be accomplished by trying to squeeze the writing in between other more important activities. Researchers who have not established a writing schedule must reorganize their priorities.

A constructive activity is to keep a record for a week or two of how time is being spent. Four unbroken hours a week or two two-hour blocks of time is adequate for getting a manuscript written. Unless a personal problem is being experienced, for example, a financial crisis or an illness, researchers are able to establish a schedule of at least four hours per week. Other time schedules are, of course, possible. For example, in the university setting many of the hours when the university is not in session can be used for writing.

Arranging a Physical Environment Conducive to Writing

Having a suitable place for writing contributes to success. The place may be an office at work or a space at home. Data and other material collected for the study, and resources for writing, including a dictionary, a thesaurus, and a guide to research writing are at hand. A bookcase and a file cabinet help organize the area.

The place for writing should permit uninterrupted work for at least two to four hours once or more per week. One's family and colleagues will probably understand the need for this and will provide support and encouragement.

Selecting a Journal

Editors of journals in education reported that they rejected as many as half of the manuscripts they received because the manuscripts were not written for their audiences–the subject matter of the manuscripts did not fit that of the journals (Henson, 1999). Authors attending annual conventions of the American Psychological Association participated in a question-and-answer session on preparing manuscripts for journal submission. The questions raised most often dealt with selecting an appropriate journal (American Psychological Association, 1997).

Selecting a journal that covers the subject matter of a researcher's study is of highest priority. Other matters to be considered are the manuscript acceptance rate, whether manuscripts are refereed, turnaround time, and manuscript length. To get this and other information that might be needed it is appropriate to proceed as follows:

1. Survey comprehensive sources of information on journals and make a tentative selection of possible journals.
2. Overview the journals tentatively selected and make a final selection.
3. Study articles in recent issues of the selected journal.
4. Contact the journal editor if further information is desired.

Journals in Psychology: A Resource Listing for Authors (American Psychological Association, 1997) supplies information on 355 journals in which half or more of the content is psychological. For each journal, the book gives the publisher and editor; editorial policy, including refereed status and kind of research and type of subject matter covered; editorial style and number of manuscript copies to submit; rejection rate if available; and other descriptive information. Some journals choose not to provide their rates; others have started recently and have not established rates. Henson (1999) identified journals that publish articles in education with 50 percent or more of the content devoted to research. Appendix B presents a list of psychology and education journals published in the English language, grouped according to content covered and rejection rates.

The subject matter covered by research journals in psychology, education, and related fields can also be surveyed by examining the abstracts of journal articles. *Psychological Abstracts,* published by the American Psychological Association, scans some 1,400 journals in the behavioral and social sciences. The electronic version of *Psychological Abstracts* (http:/www.apa.org//psycinfo/products/psycabs.html) is produced by PsycINFO, a department of APA. *Psychological Abstracts* is updated monthly. Complete journal articles along with their abstracts and other information are available electronically (http://www.apa.org/journals/homepage.html).

The second step in selecting a journal is to get an overview of the journals tentatively selected and make a final selection. Each issue of a research journal typically gives the type of research published, for example, empirical studies or research reviews; the kind of subject matter covered; manuscript requirements, for example, length and number of copies to be submitted; editorial style; and other information. Excerpts from an educational research journal and a psychological journal show this type of content.

American Educational Research Journal (Volume 36, Number 2–Summer, 1999, inside cover).

> American Educational Research Journal (ISSN 0002-8312) is published quarterly (spring, summer, fall, winter). . .to carry original reports of empirical and theoretical studies and analyses in education. . . .

> **Instructions to Contributors.** Five fully blinded copies of the manuscript should be submitted (see the Publication Manual of the American Psychological Association, 4th ed., 1994, for an example) for blind reviewing. The manuscript should be typed double-spaced (including quotations, footnotes, and references) on 8-1/2 x 11 in. paper with ample margins, and should run between 20 and 50 pages in typed length. The author's name and affiliation should appear on a separate cover page, and only on this page, to ensure anonymity in the reviewing process. An abstract of 100-150 words should be included on a separate page. Manuscripts are accepted for consideration with the understanding that they are original material and are not under consideration for publication elsewhere. . . .

Editorial review usually takes 3-4 months. Language and format must conform either to the *Publication Manual of the American Psychological Association* (4th ed., 1994) or to *The Chicago Manual of Style* (14th ed., 1993). All figures must be camera-ready. Manuscripts not conforming to these specifications will be returned to the author for proper style change.

Journal of Educational Psychology (Volume 92, Number 1, 2000, inside cover).

> The main purpose of the *Journal of Educational Psychology* is to publish original, primary psychological research pertaining to education at every educational level, from interventions during early childhood to educational efforts directed at elderly adults. A secondary purpose of the *Journal* is the occasional publication of exceptionally important theoretical and review articles directly pertinent to educational psychology. The scope of coverage of the Journal articles includes, but is not limited to, scholarship on learning, cognition, instruction, motivation, social issues, emotion, development, special populations (e.g., students with learning disabilities), individual differences in teachers, and individual differences in learners. . . .

> **Manuscripts.** Submit five copies of manuscripts to the Editor, Michael Pressley, Department of Psychology, University of Notre Dame, Notre Dame, Indiana, 46556, according to the Instructions to Authors published elsewhere in this issue.

The Instructions to Authors include the following points:

- Manuscripts should be prepared according to the *Publication Manual of the American Psychological Association* (4th ed.).
- The manuscript must not be submitted to other publications and must present original data.
- Authors are required to state in writing that they have complied with APA ethical standards in the treatment of their sample.
- The manuscript will be submitted to masked review.
- Five copies of the manuscript should be submitted.
- All copies should be clear, readable, and on paper of good quality.

More information is given regarding the preceding points. The *Journal* also supplies information on the availability of reprints, price of back issues and back volumes, change of address of authors, and journal staff and editors.

The third step in journal selection is to study a few articles in recent issues of the journal. This will assure a researcher that it publishes the kind of subject matter of the study. It will also help with writing style, evaluating the quality of the content of the study, organizing a manuscript, generating headings, and preparing tables and figures. Moreover, relevant articles may be found that were not included in the review of the literature. Adding them to the review will increase the prospects for getting a manuscript accepted.

The last step in journal selection is to contact the editor of the selected journal if further information is desired about any aspect of the selection process. In fact, an editor might be contacted at any prior step to get otherwise unavailable information about the subject matter covered by a journal or its rejection rate.

Preparing an Outline

Preparing an outline requires generating the main parts and subparts of a manuscript and composing appropriate headings. The organization of an empirical study in itself suggests three main headings: *Method, Results,* and *Discussion.* The heading *Introduction* is not used. The introduction typically includes the review of the literature and the statement of the problem.

As indicated earlier, examination of articles in recent issues of the journal selected to publish a study will help in preparing an outline for a manuscript, including its organization and related headings. Journal articles use from one to five levels of headings to indicate main points and subpoints. Most articles use two, three, or four levels. Chapter 5 provides outlines of research reports organized with headings of these three levels.

Planning to Meet Manuscript Length Requirements

Meeting a journal's requirement regarding manuscript length is difficult, especially for dissertation authors and researchers whose studies are comprehensive, for example, longitudinal studies and studies having multiple independent and dependent variables. Preparing more than one manuscript and presenting material more concisely may solve the length problem.

Preparing More Than One Manuscript

A manuscript may be written that summarizes and highlights the substance of a study. This kind of manuscript requires providing an introduction in which the problem is stated and the literature is reviewed, describing the method, giving the results, and presenting a discussion.

A second manuscript may focus on clarifying a theory. Here the literature reviewed in a study supplies the substance for most of the manuscript. The results provide the main basis for clarification of the theory. In this kind of manuscript, relatively little space is given to the methods or the findings.

A third manuscript may be a review of the literature. It will summarize the literature included in the study and also literature reflecting other points of view. An analysis of all the literature will be presented. It is especially important that the analysis brings new ideas into the field.

Favoring Brevity and Conciseness

Meeting a journal's requirement regarding manuscript length poses a difficulty for most manuscript authors. Taking the following into account when planning to write a manuscript will contribute to its being concise and as brief as possible.

Narrow the problem area. A study has a central problem and also peripheral problems. A manuscript based on this study should focus on the central problem. The peripheral problems should be mentioned only briefly, if at all. If the results pertaining to the peripheral problems are indeed important, preparation of a second manuscript may be in order.

State the problem concisely. Researchers often provide more information than is needed to state the problem and clarify its importance. The excess information is presented to show that the study makes a very important contribution to clarifying a theory, improving practice, or both. Despite the significant contributions the study may make, the presentation must be limited to paragraphs rather than pages.

Make the literature review brief. In a manuscript reporting an empirical study, the literature review must be kept short. This is done by giving only a sentence or two to a study that relates directly to the problem. Only the most important common element of several less critical studies is cited in one sentence rather than giving a sentence, a paragraph, or more to each one. The surnames of the several authors and the publication dates are enclosed in parentheses.

Obsolescent studies must not be included in the review. To illustrate, in the dissertation an author properly documented the development of a theory from the first article on it in 1966 through the most recent articles updating aspects of the theory. In the manuscript based on the dissertation, the author included the recent references and only those less recent that contributed directly to clarifying the updated version of the theory.

Include only the essentials of the method. A study has three groups of participants that receive different, lengthy instructions. The participants are administered a pretest, a posttest, and a transfer test, each having 50 multiple-choice items. Neither the instructions nor the tests are put in the manuscript. Instead, the instructions are summarized and a short segment from each one is quoted. In a few sentences, the three tests and their administration are described and an item from each test is provided. Tests and instructions that must be reproduced are put in an appendix.

Be selective in presenting and discussing the results. A study included seven null hypotheses. Two were rejected at the .05 level of statistical significance. The levels for the other five ranged from .09 to .15. In the results chapter, the dissertation author briefly discussed the two hypotheses significant at the .05 level but presented lengthy discussions of the others. Testing conditions and features of the distribution of the scores that might have contributed to the lack of significance were presented. Trends were inferred and other tangential information was given.

Failure to reject the five null hypotheses may have contributed to knowledge in the field as much as rejection of the other two. In the manuscript based on the dissertation, the author might well present the five hypotheses not rejected and the related levels of significance. However, the discussion of them must be kept brief.

After analyzing a study, an author may conclude that it does not justify a full-length article. Some journals publish short articles of one to three journal pages in a section called a *Brief Report*. A brief report usually gives only the method and the results. Selecting a journal for a brief report entails the same considerations as for other articles.

The effort required to develop a plan for writing a manuscript varies among authors. Whether devoting one work session or several to planning, the payoff is large. Many hours of searching, writing, and revising are saved. Seeing the manuscript take form and eventually getting reprints of the article are exciting career milestones.

Chapter 3

WRITING STYLE, GRAMMAR, AND BIAS IN LANGUAGE

The content of a manuscript must be of high quality to be accepted for publication as was indicated in Chapter 2. Journal editors also expect manuscript authors to use clear expository writing, correct grammar, and language free of bias related to sexual orientation, race and ethnicity, disabilities, gender, and aging.

Writing Style

Writing style refers to the manner in which authors convey their ideas to readers. Research journals use an expository style.

Expository writing involves sequencing ideas logically from the opening statement in the introduction of a manuscript to the conclusion. This implies that the parts of a manuscript follow one another in an orderly sequence. Also, the paragraphs are unified. Every sentence of a paragraph presents information directly related to the paragraph topic. Words throughout the manuscript provide for continuity and transition, express thoughts concisely, and convey meanings precisely.

Sequence the Parts of a Manuscript Logically

Presenting material logically enhances reader comprehension. The sequence for reporting a research study is in itself logical:

1. Introduce the problem, review the literature, connect the two, and state the hypothesis or the research question.
2. Describe the method–participants, materials, and procedure.
3. Present the results.
4. Discuss the results and offer implications.

Readers should be able to readily understand each of the preceding parts of a report. This calls for the first paragraph of each part to be stated clearly and precisely. Ideas that may be novel to the reader and therefore not easily understood come later.

Develop Unified Paragraphs

A unified paragraph is coherent. The ideas in the sentences of the paragraph fit together substantively. The ideas in each sentence relate to the paragraph topic.

The successive sentences in a paragraph flow; that is, they link up with one another. There are no gaps in the flow of ideas; rather, there is continuity.

A unified expository paragraph starts with the topic of the paragraph, typically given in the first sentence. The remaining sentences clarify the idea expressed in the topic sentence.

Achieving coherence and smoothness in paragraphs is an important element of expository writing. Guides and examples for developing unified paragraphs follow.

Relate ideas logically with transitional words. Specific transitional words apply to particular concepts (e.g., *however* and *nevertheless* apply to the concept *contrast*). In the examples below, concepts are followed with related transitional words:

Addition.	and, also, furthermore, moreover
Cause and effect.	consequently, therefore, thus
Contrast.	although, however, nevertheless, on the other hand, still, yet
Method.	in this way, similarly
Position.	behind, beside, close to, down, here, next to, to the left of
Time.	after, before, during, finally, first, next, since, until, when, while

Avoid the omission and the faulty use of transitional words.

Omitted. The client started to cry. The therapist discontinued the procedure. (The client started to cry. Therefore? Nevertheless? the therapist discontinued the procedure.)

Unintended meaning. The sociologist conducted a survey on sexual behavior. Consequently, many respondents changed their opinions about sexual behavior.

Intended meaning. The sociologist conducted a survey on sexual behavior. Subsequently, many respondents changed their opinions.

Avoid switching the tense, voice, or subject of verbs needlessly. A unified paragraph proceeds from the first to the last sentence in an unbroken, continuous manner. There are no breaks between the sentences that weaken the flow of the paragraph.

Tense

The literature review in a research manuscript uses the past tense or the present perfect tense. The discussion of the results and the conclusions use the present tense. The tense may be switched needlessly in these and other parts of a manuscript. The examples that follow show how tense may be switched incorrectly through inattention when concentrating on the content.

Switched. Iron (1960) summarized early studies of arithmetic. More recently, Bloom (1998) reveals weaknesses in the early studies.
Corrected. Iron (1960) summarized early studies of arithmetic. More recently, Bloom (1998) revealed weaknesses in the early studies.

Switched. Examination of the results indicates progress in raising the achievement of young children. However, the results also showed no gain for children with attention deficits.
Corrected. Examination of the results indicates . . . However, the results also show no gain for children . . .

Voice

Switched. If researchers are to be successful, appropriate experimental designs must be used.
Corrected. If researchers are to be successful, they must employ appropriate experimental designs.

Switched. The psychologist changed employment. The change is agreeable to everyone.
Corrected. The psychologist changed employment. The change was agreeable to everyone.

Subject of Verb

Switched. Shortcomings in the early theories of intimacy were a reality; subjective experiences provided the only support for the theories.
Preferred. Shortcomings in the early theories of intimacy were a reality; one shortcoming was that subjective experiences provided the only support for the theories.

Switched. The statistical procedure was analysis of variance; the results were reliable.
Preferred. The statistical procedure was analysis of variance. This procedure gave reliable results.

Develop Sentences That Express Ideas Concisely, Precisely, and Logically

Conciseness implies stating much information in few words and making every word count. Wordiness, redundancy, and long sentences reduce conciseness.

Avoid wordiness. Wordiness involves using more words than are necessary to communicate meaningfully. In many instances of wordiness, two or more words can be replaced with one:

at an early date – soon	for the purpose of – for, to
at the present time – now	hold in possession – possess
based on the fact that – because	in advance of – before
consensus of opinion – consensus	rendered assistance to – assisted
during the time that – while	succumb to injuries – die
end product – result	the present study – this study

Wordy. There were several experiments that failed.
Concise. Several experiments failed.

Wordy. The data were collected in the month of June.
Concise. The data were collected in June.

Wordy. The client took his own life by intentionally shooting himself.
Concise. The client committed suicide by shooting himself.

Avoid redundancy. Redundancy, like wordiness, refers to the use of more words than is necessary. One element of a construction conveys the meaning; the other is not necessary.

follow after – follow	absolutely essential – essential
join together – join	completely unanimous – unanimous
separate apart – separate	entirely complete – complete
summarize briefly – summarize	positively correct – correct
general rule – rule	huge in size – huge
opinionated editorial – editorial	many in number – many
present incumbent – incumbent	but nevertheless – but
true fact – fact	if and when – if

Prefer brief sentences. The length of sentences merits attention in research writing. Short simple sentences are more easily read and understood than are long complex and compound sentences.

Most sentences in a research report should be no more than 20 words in length. However, longer sentences may at times contribute to conciseness. For example, a longer sentence that gives two or more conclusions may eliminate the need for two or more short simple sentences. Longer sentences often appear in abstracts and in summaries of results.

Brevity is also an important factor in paragraphs. Every paragraph should have at least two sentences. Paragraphs longer than a double-spaced typewritten page should be reorganized into two or more paragraphs.

Preciseness in developing sentences is as important as conciseness. Precise and clear writing reflects clear thinking. It calls for stating ideas accurately. Precise writing is readily understood and leaves the reader with no doubt about the author's intended meaning. Use of appropriate terminology enhances precise writing.

Prefer concrete rather than abstract terms. Concrete words name things that can be sensed: a rose, a horn blowing, coffee aroma, a baby's skin. Abstract words name ideas that have no perceptible examples: heaven, spirit, antiquity, the social order. The abstractness of words is a matter of degree. The more a word moves from the specific, the more abstract it becomes (e.g., a Peace rose, a rose, a flowering plant, a plant).

In research writing, abstract terms should be used only if there are not concrete terms that could be used instead. However, abstraction is sometimes necessary (e.g., The t-value was significant at the .05 level). Authors use various means of clarifying abstract terms, especially for readers who are unfamiliar with the subject matter. They give a definition of the word, verbal examples, and synonyms. They explain how the word is used.

The examples that follow show how sentences can be rewritten to use concrete instead of abstract terms. The concrete terms convey the message more precisely:

Abstract	Concrete
The adult patients relaxed.	The male and female patients relaxed.
The client displayed emotions.	The client displayed love and affection.
Figure 1 showed geometric figures.	Figure 1 showed triangles and squares.
The objective test items were easy.	The multiple-choice items were easy.

Choose words that convey the precise meaning. The mass media use many words incorrectly. Researchers hear the faulty usage and, unless careful, introduce it into their writing. Many nouns, verbs, and adjectives, including those that follow, are often not used precisely:

ability/capacity	can/may	anxious/eager
accident/mishap	convince/persuade	better/best
affect/effect	flaunt/flout	bimonthly/semimonthly
allusion/illusion	lay/lie	capital/capitol
alternate/alternative	shall/will	discreet/discrete
bias/prejudice		farther/further
complement/compliment		fewer/less
connotation/denotation		ingenious/ingenuous
diagnosis/prognosis		optimistic/hopeful
foreword/forward		oral/verbal
majority/plurality		practicable/practical
mania/phobia		stationary/stationery
people/persons		tactile/tactual
principle/principal		

Make the referents of simple pronouns clear. Simple pronouns include *this* and *that*. Faulty use of simple pronouns occurs frequently at the beginning of a sentence.

> **Unclear.** The preliminary results had implications for practitioners. These were considered by the audience.
> **Clear.** The preliminary results had implications for the practitioners. These results were considered by the audience.

Unclear. The patient committed a major felony and lied about it. That was considered unconscionable.

Clear. The patient committed a major felony and lied about it. That felony was considered unconscionable.

Avoid noun strings. Noun strings are formed by placing two or more nouns together. The earlier noun or nouns are used as adjectives.

Strung together. Smith (1997) carried out a control experiment method.

Preferred. Smith (1997) carried out a controlled experiment.

Strung together. Jules (1999) reported that the men deficiency graduates were widowers.

Preferred. Jules (1999) reported that the graduates with deficiencies were widowers.

Use punctuation to show logical relationships. Punctuation helps the reader delineate logical relationships. Notice the relationships in this sentence: "The discussion pointed to three ways of gathering data: testing, measuring, and interviewing." Here the colon divides the sentence into two main parts: the introductory generalization and a list of specific examples. The commas mark each example. The period completes the expression. The logical relationships made clear by the punctuation facilitate reader comprehension.

In summary, developing unified paragraphs is the key to effective expository writing. This is difficult for many writers. As a means of improving their writing, they analyze their completed work. The analysis of the procedure section of a manuscript illustrates the process.

First, consider the topic sentence of each paragraph to make sure that it relates directly to the procedure. If it does not, rewrite the sentence or delete the paragraph if it presents information unrelated to the procedure.

Second, starting with the first paragraph of the procedure section, check each sentence of the paragraph to ascertain whether it deals with the paragraph topic. If it does not, either rewrite or delete it. However, if the sentence contains essential information, develop it into a topic sentence and construct a new paragraph. Be aware that coherence and flow are more readily attained in shorter than in longer paragraphs.

Third, read the paragraphs aloud. Reorder sentences within a paragraph if this results in increased coherence or a smoother presentation. If problems are found, consider implementing guides presented earlier in this chapter.

Grammar

Correct grammar and logical sentence structure make reading easier and foster clear communication. Conversely, incorrect grammar and faulty sentence structure divert the reader's attention and also result in ambiguity. The guides and examples that follow help writers avoid frequently occurring errors.

Nouns

Grammar pertaining to nouns deals with the agreement of nouns and verbs in number (singular and plural). The guides dealing with agreement are presented later in the section on verbs.

Pronouns

Pronouns take the place of nouns. Writers have more difficulty with pronouns than nouns.

Avoid faulty use of *that* and *which*. *That* is used to begin a restrictive clause; *which* to begin either a restrictive or a nonrestrictive clause.

Restrictive. The study that preceded this one was completed in 1998.

Restrictive. The research which was most significant had participants of all races.

Nonrestrictive. Our research, which was supported by a foundation, contributed to theory development.

Avoid faulty use of the nominative and the objective case of pronouns. Use the nominative case when a pronoun is the subject of a verb; use the objective case when a pronoun is the object of a verb or a preposition.

Incorrect. The participant whom you selected became ill.
Correct. The participant who you selected became ill.

Incorrect. The client who you identified as Jim . . .
Correct. The client whom you identified as Jim . . .

Incorrect. The experiment was designed by she and I.
Correct. The experiment was designed by her and me.

Make an indefinite pronoun and the noun it replaces agree in number. Indefinite pronouns include *all, any, few, more, none,* and many others. *None* is especially troublesome.

Meaning a group. The research team invited its colleagues.

Meaning individuals. The research team invited their colleagues.

Meaning no amount. None of the time was spent in conferences.

Meaning not one. None of the children were ill.

Make a personal pronoun and the noun it replaces agree in gender.

Male. Cardinal Bernardin wrote his memoirs.

Female. Diana loved her children.

Neuter. The play that had its character . . .

Use the possessive case of a pronoun that precedes a present participle used as a noun.

Incorrect. John accepted a notice about him accepting leadership.
Correct. John accepted a notice about his accepting leadership.

Incorrect. The participants had nothing to do with them being chosen.
Correct. The participants had nothing to do with their being chosen.

Avoid errors related to the possessive case of indefinite pronouns.

Incorrect. Everyone completed their interviews.

Awkward. Everyone completed his/her interviews.
        Everyone completed his or her interviews.

Preferred. All of the counselors completed their interviews.

Wherever possible, change *his/her* to the preferred *their*. Examine articles in the journal to which you will send your manuscript. The journal may accept usage such as "everyone completed their interviews."

Verbs and Verbal Phrases

The earlier discussion of clarity and precision stressed consistency related to the tense, voice, and subject of verbs. Here we consider grammar.

There are three verb forms: participles, gerunds, and infinitives. A verbal phrase consists of verb form and one or more other words (e.g., *Answering quickly*, the client . . .; *Answering quickly* led to errors; *To answer correctly*, the participant . . .). Implementing the following guides related to verbs and verbal phrases heightens the reader's interest and improves the clarity of a research report.

Prefer the active voice.

Passive. The study was designed appropriately.
Active. The researcher designed the study appropriately.

Passive. Educational implications are offered in this study.
Active. This study offers educational implications.

Prefer verbs rather than nouns and verbal phrases used as nouns.

Problematic. The social worker engaged in a conversation with the child's father.
Preferred. The social worker conversed with the child's father.

Problematic. Steven did a replication of Burt's study.
Preferred. Steven replicated Burt's study.

Problematic. Sarah completed conducting her experiment.
Preferred. Sarah completed her experiment.

Problematic. Suzanne decided to initiate a referral.
Preferred. Suzanne initiated a referral.

Make a verb agree in number with its subject.

Incorrect. The prospect of more deaths increases as the incidence of depression and alcoholism increase.
Correct. The prospect of more deaths increases as the incidence of depression and alcoholism increases.

Incorrect. The data shows that only one student was Asian American.
Correct. The data show that only one student was Asian American.

Make a verb agree in number with the noun closer to the verb when the subject of a sentence is both a singular noun and a plural noun.

> **Incorrect.** Either the true-false questions or the essay question were of low reliability.
> **Correct.** Either the true-false questions or the essay question was of low reliability.

> **Incorrect.** Neither the man nor the women was ready.
> **Correct.** Neither the man nor the women were ready.

Retain the verb of each clause when the subject of the clauses changes in number.

> **Incorrect.** The patients were bathed and dinner served.
> **Correct.** The patients were bathed and dinner was served.

> **Incorrect.** The test was ready and the students eager to take it.
> **Correct.** The test was ready and the students were eager to take it.

Avoid both dangling and misplaced verb forms. A dangling modifier has no referent in a sentence; however, it may seem to modify a word, thereby giving an unintended meaning. A misplaced modifier ambiguously or illogically modifies a word in a sentence.

> **Dangling.** After looking closely into the causes of the failure, the children were excused by the teacher.
> **Corrected.** After looking closely into the causes of the failures, the teacher excused the children.

> **Dangling.** The therapist counseled the students using a nondirective procedure.
> **Corrected.** The therapist, using a nondirective procedure, counseled the students.

> **Dangling.** To save time, the students were given numbers.
> **Corrected.** To save time, the experimenter gave the students numbers.

> **Misplaced.** The examiner, when entering the library, told the participants to be quiet.
> **Corrected.** The examiner told the participants to be quiet when entering the library.

Misplaced. The psychologist ignored the students being nondirective.
Corrected. The psychologist, being nondirective, ignored the students.

Choose the subjunctive mood for particular expressions. The subjunctive mood is rarely used in spoken English and not often in written English. However, in research reporting, it is used in expressing a wish, a condition contrary to fact, and in a few other contexts.

To indicate a wish. If the researcher were not White . . .

To indicate contrary to the fact. The client wished that the therapist were there.

In a clause introduced by "if." An experimenter proceeded as if he were not expecting to accept the hypothesis.

Traditional idioms and phrases. Be that as it may, come what may, if I were you, so be it.

Adjectives and Adverbs

Adjectives and adverbs are modifiers that add detailed information (e.g., *empirical* study, ran *slowly*). Verb phrases may be used as adjectives (e.g., *Answering quickly*, the participants made many errors); or as adverbs (e.g., the patient called *to verify an appointment*).

Adhere to the conventional use of introductory adjectives, introductory adverbs, and connecting adverbs.

Problematic. More importantly, the evidence suggests innocence.
Preferred. More important, the evidence suggests innocence.

Problematic. Hopefully, the victim will survive.
Preferred. The parents hope the victim will survive.

Problematic. The test validity was low; similarly, the test reliability was low.
Preferred. The test reliability was low; consequently, the test validity was low.

Avoid giving an unintended meaning by misplacing an adjective or an adverb.

> **Unintended meaning.** The participant observed the therapist as an uninterested bystander.
> **Intended meaning.** The participant, as an uninterested bystander, observed the therapist.

> **Unintended meaning.** The examiner almost duplicated all of the tests.
> **Intended meaning.** The examiner duplicated almost all of the tests.

> **Unintended meaning.** The social workers only recorded the clients' home conditions.
> **Intended meaning.** The social workers recorded only the clients' home conditions.

Use *while* and *since* to refer only to the concept of time.

Problematic. Mary gave high ratings, while Ashley rated items low.
Preferred. Mary gave high ratings, whereas Ashley rated items low.

Problematic. The data were flawed since two participants cheated.
Preferred. The data were flawed because two participants cheated.

Prepositions and Prepositional Phrases

A preposition shows a relationship between the object of a preposition and some other word in a sentence. A prepositional phrase is a sequence of words that starts with a preposition. A prepositional phrase may modify a noun or a verb.

Avoid errors in the choice of prepositions.

> **Incorrect.** The forms were distributed between 20 boys.
> **Correct.** The forms were distributed among 20 boys.

> **Incorrect.** The teacher sat besides the child.
> **Correct.** The teacher sat beside the child.

> **Incorrect.** Essay tests, as interviews, often have low reliability.
> **Correct.** Essay tests, like interviews, often have low reliability.

Avoid giving an unintended meaning by misplacing a preposition-al phrase.

> **Unintended meaning.** The patient took a sedative from Ward C.
> **Intended meaning.** The patient from Ward C took a sedative.

> **Unintended meaning.** The test copies were distributed to the students with answer sheets.
> **Intended meaning.** The test copies with answer sheets were distributed to the students.

> **Unintended meaning.** The psychologist met to consider rentals and the increasing cost of living with women.
> **Intended meaning.** The psychologist met with women to consider rentals and the increasing cost of living.

Follow some words with specific prepositions. The next examples include a few of many prepositions and related specific words:

> **From.** aloof, different, emigrate, excerpt, inseparable, separate
> **In.** interest, involve, lacking, participate, place (in, not into)
> **Of.** disapproval, distrustful, possibility, recognition
> **To.** complementary, dissimilar, hindrance, incidental, liken, opposition
> **With.** coincident, contemporary, habitual, incongruous, inconsistent

Conjunctions

There are two kinds of conjunctions: coordinating and subordinating. Coordinating conjunctions (e.g., *and, but*) connect elements of equal rank. Some coordinating conjunctions are correlative (e.g., *either/or, neither/nor*). Subordinating conjunctions (e.g., *but that, so that*) connect elements of unequal rank. By being inattentive or by feeling rushed, authors sometimes make mistakes in using conjunctions.

Avoid omitting a coordinating conjunction. Coordinating conjunctions include *and, but, or, nor, so.*

> **Incorrect.** The psychologist interviewed the child, recorded the results.
> **Correct.** The psychologist interviewed the child and recorded the results.

Incorrect. The examiner supplied test copies, pencils, erasers, paper, written instructions.

Correct. The examiner supplied test copies, pencils, erasers, paper, and written instructions. (Without *and* the implication is that the examiner supplied other items also.)

Avoid misplacing correlative conjunctions. *Both/and, either/or, neither/nor,* and *not only/but also* are correlating conjunctions.

Misplaced. The therapist neither prescribed drugs nor exercise.

Correct. The therapist prescribed neither drugs nor exercise.

Misplaced. The participants responded both in English and French.

Correct. The participants responded in both English and French. (Another correct way: The participants responded both in English and in French.)

Avoid faulty use of subordinating conjunctions. *But that, but what, so that, that which, since, while, when* and *where* are subordinating conjunctions.

Unintended meaning. The therapist cannot see that the child's progress is satisfactory.

Intended. The therapist cannot see but that the child's progress is satisfactory. (The meaning here is directly opposite to the unintended meaning.)

Unclear meaning. The psychologists studied so they would be granted a license.

Clear. The psychologists studied so that they would be granted a license.

Express Ideas in Parallel Form

Parallel construction contributes to the accuracy of expression. It shows relationships clearly between elements within sentences and ideas among sentences. Conjunctions contribute to parallelism.

Express items of a series in parallel form.

Not parallel. Empathy, sympathy, and being kind contribute to a patient's good will.

Parallel. Empathy, sympathy, and kindness contribute to a patient's good will.

Not parallel. Testing, measuring, and interviews with participants are means of gathering data.
Parallel. Testing, measuring, and interviewing participants are means of gathering data.

Express elements within a sentence and ideas among sentences in parallel form.

Not parallel. The experimenter instructed the participants to be quiet and they should try hard.
Parallel. The experimenter instructed the participants to be quiet and to try hard.

Not parallel. The researcher was more interested in planning and designing the study than to implement it.
Parallel. The researcher was more interested in planning and designing the study than in implementing it.

Not parallel. The therapist offered two suggestions: first, discontinue Vitamin E for two days and lessen the calorie intake; second, weight was to be taken both morning and evening.
Parallel. The therapist offered two suggestions: first, discontinue Vitamin E for two days and lessen the calorie intake; second, take weight both morning and evening.

Express the names of women and men in parallel form.

Not parallel. Joseph Smith and Geraldine
Parallel. Joseph Smith and Geraldine Smith, Joseph and Geraldine Smith, Joseph and Geraldine

Bias in Language

The American Psychological Association (APA) has exercised strong leadership in encouraging authors to eliminate bias in language. APA commissions have developed rationales and proposals that deal with eliminating bias. The guides that follow are in line with the recommendations given in publications of the American Psychological Association: *Guidelines for Nonsexist Language in APA Journals* (1977, June), *Guidelines for Avoiding Racial/Ethnic Bias in Language* (1989), *Avoiding Heterosexual Bias in Language* (1991), *Guidelines for Nonhandicapping Language in APA Journals* (1992b), and

Publication Manual of APA (1994). *The Dictionary of Bias-Free Usage: A Guide to Nondiscriminatory Language* (Maggio, 1991) lists many discriminatory terms and gives nondiscriminatory substitutes.

Avoid Bias Related to Sexual Orientation

Public opinion regarding sexual orientation has changed in recent decades. Attitudes are more realistic and there is more openness about sexual behavior that is not heterosexual. However, bias continues. Authors have a special responsibility for using language that does not contribute to negative bias.

Prefer the term *sexual orientation* rather than *sexual preference*. *Sexual orientation* refers to the sexual relationships of lesbian, gay male, bisexual, and heterosexual people. *Sexual preference* implies that people voluntarily choose their sexual behavior. However, the choice may not be voluntary inasmuch as heredity and involuntary environmental conditions affect a person's sexual orientation.

> **Incorrect.** Robert's conversation with the therapist implied a male-male sexual preference.
> **Preferred.** Robert's conversation with the therapist implied a male-male sexual orientation.

Prefer the terms *lesbians* and *gay men* rather than *homosexuals*. Using the word *homosexual* perpetuates a negative stereotype of lesbians and gay men. Some people regard homosexuality as criminal or sinful. Too, homosexuality is sometimes assumed to refer exclusively to gay men.

> **Stereotypic.** In the follow-up study, the men behaved like homosexuals.
> **Non-stereotypic.** In the follow-up study, the men behaved like male-male partners.

Avoid faulty use of the terms *male-male sexual behavior* and *female-female sexual behavior*. These terms apply not only to the same-gender sexual behavior of gay men and lesbians but also to the same-gender sexual behavior of people, regardless of their sexual orientation. Some men and women have same-gender sexual relationships but do not consider themselves to be gay men or lesbians.

Biased. The researcher saw a news account that said that a gay married man with children was engaging in extramarital male-male sexual relationships.

Not-biased. The researcher saw a news account that said that a married man with children who did not consider himself gay was engaging in extramarital male-male sexual relationships.

Avoid the use of *sexual deviation, sexual inversion,* and similar demeaning terms.

Demeaning. The therapist introduced a sexual deviate to the audience.

Non-demeaning. The therapist introduced a gay man to the audience.

For decades, the term *sex* appeared in the research literature to designate male and female gender (e.g., the researcher reported differences between the sexes in mathematical achievements). Presently, reference to males and females employs the term *gender* (e.g., the researcher reported gender differences in mathematical achievements).

Avoid Bias Related to Race and Ethnicity

Bias related to race and ethnicity may be shown by improperly selecting participants, comparing groups unfairly, drawing unfair conclusions, or using language that reflects bias. Although all of these are important considerations, the guides that follow are limited to eliminating bias in language and making unfair comparisons of groups.

Designate a racial or an ethnic group by the name it prefers. Selection of a name may be difficult inasmuch as groups change their names from time to time. Furthermore, leaders of a group do not always agree on a preferred name.

Preferred. Black or African American rather than Negro or Afro-American

Preferred. Native American or American Indian rather than Indian

Preferred. Asian or Asian American rather than Oriental

Preferred subgroup. Navajo people or Navajo nation rather than American Indian

Preferred subgroup. Japanese rather than Asians

You may note that the multiword names are not hyphenated and that *Black* is capitalized. *White* should also be capitalized.

Specify precisely the participants' race or ethnicity.

Imprecise. The researcher compared the profiles of 100 adolescents.
Precise. The researcher compared the profiles of 50 Black and 50 White adolescents.

Imprecise. The psychologist tried the procedure with children living below the poverty line.
Precise. The psychologist tried the procedure with 10 Jewish and 10 Puerto Rican children living below the poverty line.

Avoid comparing groups and using modifying terms that may elicit biased conclusions.

Biased comparison. Of the admissions to the 1998 university freshman class, 80% were White and Asian American whereas only 20% were Black and Hispanic. (Some readers may infer that White and Asian American students in general are more academically able than are Black and Hispanic students.)

Biased modifier. The talented Jewish professor gained widespread recognition. (A reader may infer that Jewish professors in general are not talented.)

Avoid Bias Related to Disabilities

Both *disability* and *handicap* refer to a physical or a mental impairment. However, a handicap for a disabled person may be an architectural, legal, or physical barrier. The barrier, not the individual's disability, handicaps or impairs the individual's performance (e.g., prejudice handicaps people with disabilities from getting jobs that they can perform competently).

Avoid using a term that implies total impairment.

Biased. Students who are educationally retarded
Preferred. Students who are mathematically retarded

Biased. A child who is physically handicapped
Preferred. A child who has had a hand amputated

Avoid labels that equate people with their disabilities.

Biased. Arthritics
Preferred. People with arthritis

Biased. The disabled
Preferred. People with disabilities

Avoid expressions that have a negative connotation.

Biased. Victims of paralysis
Preferred. People who are paralyzed

Biased. Polio sufferers
Preferred. People with polio

Biased. People cursed with AIDS
Preferred. People with AIDS

Biased. People afflicted with heart disease
Preferred. People with heart disease

Avoid Bias Related to Gender

A policy of the American Psychological Association requires writers of manuscripts to avoid language that could be construed as sexist. Presently, not only all APA journals but also many others implement this policy.

Prefer using unbiased terminology.

Biased	Unbiased
aggressive male and timid female participants	male and female participants
chairman	chair, chairperson
man, mankind	humankind, human race, human species, humanity, human beings, people
manpower	workforce, workers, personnel

man's use of force	people's use of force
man the project	hire personnel, employ staff
scientists and their wives	scientists and their spouses
the home of Mrs. Jane Smith	the home of Jane Smith
the office girls	assistants, receptionists, secretaries

Avoid faulty use of modifiers.

Faulty	**Preferred**
a woman doctor and a lady social worker	a female doctor and a female social worker
adolescent boy participants	adolescent male participants

Avoid Bias Related to Aging

Schaie (1993) indicated that bias related to aging is especially important because of the rapidly increasing number of older people. Also, policy makers are giving more attention to research on aging.

A researcher may introduce age bias at any point in a study, starting with identifying a problem through interpreting the results. The focus here is on eliminating bias when preparing a manuscript for publication.

When referring to older participants, some writers use negative stereotyping language (e.g., *decline, dependency, deterioration, disability*). Also, they use terminology that implies that older people are care needing rather than care providing.

In reporting results, some writers give generalizations only; they ignore individual differences. However, differences are probably greater among older than younger people. Ignoring individual differences and thereby stereotyping is a main problem in research on older people (Schaie, 1993).

> **Stereotypic.** Group A was a healthy younger group under age 50. Group B was a declining older group over age 60.
> **Non-stereotypic.** Group A was a younger group under age 50. Group B was an older group over age 60.

Stereotypic. Group A, over age 62, were Medicaid dependents.
Non-stereotypic. Group A, over age 62, were receiving their health care through Medicaid.

Stereotypic. Social workers should expect the clients above age 60 to experience a rapid decline in memory.
Non-stereotypic. Social workers should expect some clients above age 60 to experience a rapid decline in memory.

Stereotypic. Some participants above age 60 are out of step with the times.
Non-stereotypic. Some participants above age 60 do not observe current trends.

This section of the chapter does not provide an exclusive list of biased terms. However, it highlights the fact that language is powerful and writers need to examine the words they use so they do not unknowingly perpetuate negative stereotypes.

Chapter 4

PUNCTUATION, CAPITALIZATION, SPELLING, HYPHENATION, ITALICS, ABBREVIATIONS, AND SERIATION

Editorial style refers to the rules or guidelines that a publisher demands of writers. Editorial style for research writing involves rules of punctuation, capitalization, abbreviation, and other mechanics of writing. These rules with examples are supplied in this chapter.

Publishers also have a style for other elements of a research manuscript, including statistical and mathematical material, figures and tables, in-text citations and references in the reference list. The style for these and other elements is dealt with in Chapters 5-7 and Appendix A. Most journals in psychology, education, and related fields follow the style given in Chapters 4-6. However, with very few exceptions, they adhere either to the style given in the *Publication Manual of the American Psychological Association* (Chapter 7) or to that in *The Chicago Manual of Style* (Appendix A), not to both.

Punctuation

Punctuation may be divided into two categories: stops and other marks. Stops signal pauses in communication. The stops are the period, question mark, colon, semicolon, comma, and dash. Other marks do not signal stops: the parenthesis, bracket, quotation mark, apostrophe, ellipsis, and slash.

Period and Question Mark

One use of periods and question marks is at the end of sentences. In this chapter, I indicate other uses of a period in abbreviations, ellipsis points, quotation marks, and parentheses; in later chapters in citations in the text and references in the reference list.

Colon

Use a colon

in ratios and proportions.

The proportion (wins:losses) was 8:5.

to precede a list or a summary.

The study examined the following sexual orientations: male-female and female-female.

to precede a final phrase or clause that clarifies or amplifies what precedes the colon.

The researcher had two concerns: the transience of the children and the poverty of their parents.

between the place of publication and the name of the publisher.

Springfield, IL: Charles C Thomas.

Do not use a colon after the last word of an incomplete sentence that precedes a quotation.

A development specialist, after reviewing the literature, suggested that "concept development proceeds more gradually than is predicted by traditional stage theories." (p. 15).

Semicolon

Use a semicolon

to separate independent clauses when they are not joined by a conjunction.

The participants in the first experiment were adolescents; those in the second experiment were children.

to separate elements of a series that contains commas.

The combination flavors in a taste experiment were peach, pear, and plum; peach, pear, and cherry; and peach, pear, and grape.

between independent clauses of a compound sentence when the clauses are linked by *accordingly, however, indeed,* or other conjunctive adverbs.

The results were ambiguous; however, they were widely quoted.

outside closing quotation marks and after a closing parenthesis.

The client said "hello"; then he left.

The study was completed by Henry (1998); it was well designed.

Comma

The comma is used to prevent misreading, to make the meaning clear, and to show relationships among elements of a sentence. Authors of informal writing and creative writing exercise wide latitude in their use of the comma. However, in scientific writing, standard rules are followed.

Use a comma

between elements in a series of three or more items, including before the last item that precedes *and* or *or.*

The interview provided information about four kinds of intimacy: emotional, intellectual, sexual, and social.

to set off a nonrestrictive clause.

A test, which had been constructed locally, had low reliability.

to separate independent clauses joined by a conjunction.

The men had become successful in the workplace, and the home is where the women excelled.

between a dependent clause and an independent clause when the dependent clause precedes the main clause.

Because the men had been raised in male environments, they were poor predictors of their wives' emotions.

in citing references and in giving exact dates.

(Weinstein, 1998); (Weinstein, 1998, reported . . .)

They set aside August 18, 1948, to start therapy.

Do not use a comma to set off a restrictive clause, between two parts of a compound predicate, or to separate parts of a measurement.

The tests that he used were easy.

Psychologists are products of society and are influenced by environmental conditions.

1 year 6 months

Dash

Use a dash

to indicate an abrupt change in a sentence.

The patients–two male nurses and three female construction workers–were released.

However, the patients–if they are dismissed they cannot be called again.

Do not use a dash when alternative marks can be used.

"What time is it? Please tell me."
The therapist responded; it was ten o'clock.
Many procedures: tests, interviews, and surveys . . .
In the book, *The Rise of Capitalism* . . .

Parentheses

Use parentheses

to set off explanatory or peripheral elements.

Acceleration is an effective means of providing for academically talented children (see Klausmeier, 1992).

to indicate citations.

Blanchard and Diamond (1996) reported . . .

to introduce abbreviations.

Committee on Gay and Lesbian Concerns (CLGC)

Personal Assessment Of Intimate Relationships (PAIR)

to enclose the letters that precede the items of a series.

The successive therapies were (a) non-directive counseling, (b) behavior modification, and (c) medication.

to enclose a citation or a page number of a direct quotation.

Helms (1997) reported that "the results were accurate" (p. 320).

The author stated, "the results were accurate" (Helms, 1997, p. 328).

Do not use parentheses back-to-back or to enclose material within parentheses.

(e.g., physical disabilities reported by Ripple & Franzen, 1986)

(The Personal Assessment Of Intimate Relationships [PAIR] was used.)

Parentheses and other punctuation marks.

• When a complete sentence is enclosed in parentheses, place the period, question mark, or exclamation point inside the parenthesis, like this.) ?) !)

- When parenthetical material that is a complete sentence is enclosed in a sentence, place the period, question mark, or exclamation point inside the parenthesis, like this.) ?) !)
- When parenthetical material that is not a complete sentence is enclosed at the end of a sentence, place the period, question mark, or exclamation point outside the parenthesis, like this)?)!
- When parenthetical material that is not a complete sentence is enclosed in a sentence, place the comma, semicolon, or colon outside the parenthesis, like this),);):

Notice the difference in the punctuation of a complete sentence enclosed in parentheses and that of parenthetical material that is not a complete sentence.

Brackets

Use brackets

to enclose parenthetical material already enclosed in parentheses.

(The participants [there should have been an equal number in each group] were 100 Asian Americans and 10 American Indians.)

to enclose material in a quotation of someone other than the original author.

"The study continued [wrote Ploss, 1998] for a period of 25 years."

"An important characteristic of learners [based on research of Snow, 1996] is how they process visual versus verbal information."

Do not use brackets where a comma might be used or to set off statistics that already include parentheses.

(Alexander, 1997, reported the study.)

significantly related to goals F (2, 203) = 5.40, p. = .01

Recognize that in mathematical material parentheses are used inside brackets.

[x = (y + 20) - (10 - z) was found to be correct.]

Quotation Marks

Use double quotation marks

to set off the title of an article or a chapter when the title is given in the text.

The article, "Motivation and Cheating in Early Childhood," presents unanticipated results.

King's (1996) chapter, "Mutual Peer Tutoring," is on the required reading list.

(Do not enclose titles in the reference list.)

to set off a test item or instructions to participants.

The essay item began, "Compare the performance of Jordan and McGuire . . .

The examiner said, "The purpose of our study is . . .

Place other punctuation marks in proper order when they are used with quotation marks. Writers often must get information on a particular punctuation mark to determine whether to place it before or after the quotation marks. They will find it helpful to refer quickly to the following correct placement of other marks:

- Place the comma and the period inside quotation marks, "like this," "like this."
- Place the semicolon and the colon outside quotation marks, "like this"; "like this":
- Place the exclamation point and the question mark inside the quotation marks when they are part of the quotation, "like this!" "Like this?"
- Place the exclamation point and question mark outside the quotation marks when they are not part of the quotation, "like this"! "Like this"?
- Place "etc." and the points of the ellipsis so that they indicate clearly whether the omitted matter is or is not part of the quotation.
- Place a comma before quotation marks when a pause is desired or when it prevents misunderstanding.

Do not use a period after a complete sentence that is enclosed in quotation marks and placed within another sentence.

The therapist's response, "I am succeeding with Harry," was questioned.

Do not use quotation marks when using a word or other construction as an example or to enclose a technical term the first time it is used.

Incorrect. Two parts of speech, "adjectives" and "adverbs" are modifiers.
Correct. Two parts of speech, adjectives and adverbs, are modifiers.

Incorrect. The statistic employed was "multiple regression."
Correct. The statistic employed was multiple regression.

Apostrophe

The apostrophe is used to show the possessive form of nouns and certain pronouns, to indicate contractions, and to form certain plurals. In some instances to show possession, an s is added after the apostrophe as will be seen in the examples.

Use an apostrophe

to show the possessive form of

singular nouns and certain pronouns that do not end in *s*.

a participant's number, a mentor's advice, anyone's report, someone's book

plural nouns that do not end in *s*.

the women's conference, the children's dance

plural nouns that end in *s*.

10 sociologists' research activities, 10 social workers' home contacts

singular compound nouns.

the son-in-law's position, the sergeant-at-arms' entry

in contractions to show the omission of letters and numbers.

he'll try, they're trying, could've–not could of, the class of '98

to form certain plurals.

the ABC's, 10 Ph.D.'s, too many but's

Do not use an apostrophe with possessive pronouns.

Hers, his, its, mine, theirs, ours, whose, yours (It's is a contraction for *it is* or *it has*.)

Ellipsis Points

Use three ellipsis points

to indicate the omission of material.

A chapter on human development began with . . . and ended with a bibliography.

"This completed the therapy. . . . The client then . . ."

to indicate an omission at the beginning or the end of a quotation or other excerpt, but only when they are necessary to prevent misinterpretation.

Slash

A frequent use of the slash is to separate the numerator from the denominator in fractions (e.g., A/B, 5/6). Faulty use of the slash includes *and/or* and *test/retest*. The preferred construction is *and* or *or* and *test-retest*.

Capitalization

There are many uses for capitals for which no one requires rules. The rules that follow are for uses that are of most importance to researchers. The examples are drawn from research reports and less formal writing.

Capitalize

a noun followed by a numeral or a letter.

The therapist completed Session 5
The participants questioned Item 20
Therapy Session A was exploratory
Schwenn was awarded Research Contract 680

the first word after a colon that begins a complete sentence.

The author made a major point: One of the most rewarding outcomes of avoiding the use of biased language is improvement in writing style.

Social workers meet a most difficult problem: Homeless adolescents getting residential treatment usually lack a traditional family and a stable support system.

proper nouns and adjectives and words used as proper nouns.

Category	Example
geographical regions	Western Europe, Pacific Coast
religious denominations and their adherents	Fundamentalists, Moslems
family appellations when used as names	I called Mother, Uncle Fred

main words in titles of articles and books within a manuscript. Verbs, nouns, adjectives, adverbs, and pronouns in titles are capitalized; articles, conjunctions, and prepositions are not, except those of four letters or more.

A recent article, "Profiling Students' Achievements"
A review of the article, "Executive Control and Achievement in Science"
The textbook, *Experimental Methods in the Behavioral Sciences*
Webster's Third New International Dictionary

only the first word and proper nouns in an indented paragraph heading.

Theories of emotional intelligence. Theorists . . .

Accounts of Thorndike's research. Thorndike . . .

name of a condition or a group in experiment.

Instructional Condition A

Experimental Group B

abbreviations of academic degrees.

B.A., M.S., Ed.D., Ph.D., Psy.D., J.D.

all the words of the title of a published or an unpublished test.

Wechsler Intelligence Scale For Children
Revised Stanford Diagnostic Arithmetic Test
The researcher developed a test, Levels Of Concept Attainment.

Do not capitalize generic and inexact titles of tests.

individual intelligence tests

Stanford arithmetic test

Spelling

For the correct spelling of a word, consult the latest edition of *Merriam-Webster's Collegiate Dictionary* or *Webster's Third New International Dictionary*. Use the first spelling listed when the dictionary gives two choices.

Hyphenation

Hyphenate

a compound construction that precedes the word it modifies.

Compound	Example
a compound with a participle	thrill-seeking activity
an adjective-and-noun compound	disadvantaged-environment condition
a phrase used as an adjective	to-be-answered item
a compound with a number as the first element	fifth-grade students
compound adjective	t-test results, male-male orientation
a compound modifier with a common base	long- and short-term memory

Hyphenate

a prefix if a base word is

a number.	pre-2000, post-1900
an abbreviation.	non-Ph.D., pre-APA
capitalized.	pro-Skinner, contra-Rogers
more than one word.	ultra-concerned child

all "self" words.

self-concept

A client was self-motivated.

Do not use a hyphen with certain prefixes.

co	coauthor, coeditor
mini	miniconference, minisession
post	postmenopause, posttest
under	underestimate, understaffed

There are many other prefixes that do not require use of the hyphen and many other self-words that do. Consult either of the dictionaries cited earlier when you have a question about hyphenation.

Italics

The use of italics increases understanding of material by distinguishing letters, words, and phrases from the rest of a sentence. Writers underline to indicate what they want italicized when the manuscript is published; they do not italicize anything.

Underline

words that could be misread (e.g., the *serious* clients, meaning a designation of a group, not a description of particular clients).

titles of periodicals and books (e.g., *Journal of Experimental Education, Introduction to Social Work*).

technical terms the first time they are used (e.g., *teaching triarchically, knowledge mapping*).

letters, words, and phrases used as examples (e.g., *1* is not used for the numeral 1; *principal* is used correctly as a noun and an adjective; *responding quickly* is a participial phrase).

letters used as statistical or algebraic variables (e.g., *t*-test, *x/y*, trial *a*).

some scale and test scores (e.g., MMPI scales–*Hs, Pd*; Rorschach scores–*Z*).

Do Not Underline

foreign phrases that are main entries in *Merriam-Webster's Collegiate Dictionary* (e.g., a priori, ad lib, et al., per se).

chemical and trigonometric terms (e.g., LSD, NA; log, sin).

letters used as abbreviations of tests (e.g., MMPI, CTMM).

letters used to indicate groups (e.g., Group B).

Abbreviations

Authors follow an established pattern when using abbreviations and acronyms in their manuscripts. They write out a term completely the first time and follow it immediately with its abbreviation in parentheses, for example, Differential Aptitude Test (DAT), National Association of Trade Organizations (NATO). They use the abbreviated form throughout the rest of the manuscript. There is an exception to the preceding. Abbreviations and acronyms that are not labeled abbr. (e.g., ESP, IQ, AIDS, UNESCO) in *Merriam-Webster's Collegiate Dictionary* are used the first time without writing out the term.

Abbreviate

technical terms and nonstandardized tests.

learning disabilities (LD)
multivariate analysis of variance (MANOVA)
Test Of Phonetic Cue Reading (TCPR)
Word-To-Word Matching Test (WWMT)
Patterns Of Adaptive Learning Survey (PALS)

Latin terms when enclosed in parentheses.

cf.	compare	i.e.	that is
e.g.	for example	viz.	namely
etc.	and so forth, and others, and the like	vs.	against, versus

units of measurement when accompanied with numbers.

10 cm, 12 min, 30 lb, 90°

(Exceptions: Do not abbreviate day, week, month, or year even when accompanied with a number, for example, 4th day, 10th week, 12th month, year 2000.)

other units of measurement.

a.m., cm, kg, min, rpm

(There are other units of measurement that are abbreviated.)

Use Periods With Abbreviations of

the United States when used as an adjective (e.g., U.S. Armed Forces).
initials for names (e.g., W. J. Clinton, J. L. Albright).
Latin terms–cf., e.g., etc., i.e., viz., vs.

Do Not Use Periods With Abbreviations of

the names of the 50 states.
acronyms that are capitalized (e.g., HOMES, WRISE).
metric and nonmetric measurements (e.g., cd, cm, lb, min).

(Exceptions: in. for inch and abbreviations for routes of administration.)

Do Not Begin a Sentence With a Lowercase Abbreviation.

Do Not Abbreviate Subject, Experiment, or Observer.

Form Plurals of Abbreviations

that have no internal periods by adding *s* only (e.g., Eds., IQs, OKs, vols., YMCAs).

that have internal periods by adding *'s* (e.g., D.D.'s, Ph.D.'s).

(Exceptions: Some abbreviations are both singular and plural [e.g., ft., doz., wk.])

For abbreviations of chemical compounds, concentrations (e.g., 1% [wt/vol] saccharin solution), or routes of administration (e.g., iv = intravenous), see American Psychological Association (1994).

Before proceeding further, be aware that the prior guides apply to abbreviations in the body of a manuscript. The use of abbreviations is somewhat different for the abstract and for statistical terms.

Seriation

Use Lowercase Letters to Mark Successive Elements in a Series of Items Within a Sentence

Use commas to separate three or more elements of a series that do not have internal commas. When the elements in a series have internal punctuation, use a semicolon to separate them.

In a unification mode of ideological operations (a) individuality is embraced, (b) a cohesive framework is promoted, and (c) a collective identity is diffused.

In a fragmentation mode of ideological operations (a) the focus is on divisions, distinctions, and aberrations; (b) an enemy, within or without, is created; and (c) any group, if capable of overt action, is dispersed.

Capitalize the First Word of the First Item of a Series When the Item Follows a Colon in a Sentence.

Ideological modes of operations have three distinctive features: (a) Reification of disabilities leads to initial rejection of groups, (b) avoidance of groups strengthens the rejection, and (c) allowing bias to remain invisible completes the rejection.

Mark Successive Paragraphs in a Series With Arabic Numerals. (The three examples are the opening words of three successive paragraphs.)

The following operations have been documented through years of research:

1. Institutional arrangements are . . .
2. A collective identity is . . .
3. A transitory state of affairs has been . . .

Notice that, different from the use of letters in a series, the numerals 1, 2, 3 are not enclosed in parentheses.

Chapter 5

NUMBERS, METRIC MEASUREMENT, STATISTICAL AND MATHEMATICAL MATERIAL, HEADINGS, AND QUOTATIONS

The material covered in this chapter is not used equally in manuscripts. For example, all manuscripts have headings but very few use metric measurements. In this chapter, reference sources, rather than guidelines, are presented for the less frequently used material.

Numbers

A widely followed rule in research writing is to use figures for numbers 10 and higher and to write out numbers below 10. This rule requires no explanation or examples. However, there are many exceptions to the rule and also special uses of figures and words that merit consideration.

Use Figures

to express numbers for age; clients and participants in a study; dates; samples, subsamples, and populations of experiments; scores; exact sums of money; and time.

16-year-old	a score of 2 on a 10-point scale
40 clients of Group A	earnings of $100
December 31, 1999	depart in 3 minutes
12 African Americans in the experiment	

to express numbers in lists that have more than three numbers, numbers indicating numbered parts of books and tables, and a specific place in a numbered series.

1, 4, 5, 9

chapter 6, page 67, column 2, Table 1
Grade 8, Psalm 23

to express fractional and decimal quantities, mathematical functions, percentiles, and ratios.

1 1/4 times as much	75th percentile
.08 of a second	a ratio of 33:2
subtracted from 278	

Use Words

to express any number that begins a heading, title, or sentence.

Three Uses of Words
Fourteen Days of Torture in Vietnam

One child was injured.
Fifty percent of the responses were correct.

to express numbers below 10 when they are grouped with numbers that are lower than 10 and do not represent exact measurements.

one of the nine	four of seven lists
two of six trials	fifth of eight trials
three-sided geometric figures	

to express common fractions.

favored by one half of the clients
two-thirds majority
one third of the participants

to express numbers in widely accepted terms.

two Houses of Parliament

July Fourth

Use a Combination of Figures and Words to Express Rounded Large Numbers and Back-to-Back Modifiers

5 million correct responses
more than 1 billion

thirty 8-year-olds
3 two-way interactions

Place a Comma Between Groups of Three Digits in Large Numbers

3,000

3,200,300

Exceptions for Comma Usage

acoustic frequency designations–3000 Hz
binary digits–0022034
degrees of freedom–F(38, 100)
degrees of temperature–1001 F

numbers after the period in a
decimal fraction–5.0812
page numbers–page 1080
serial numbers–5618

Add s or es Without an Apostrophe to Form the Plural of Figures and Words Representing Numbers

10s, 2000s

forties, nineties

Use Figures and Words to Represent Ordinal Numbers in the Same Way as Cardinal Numbers

the first item of the test
the 10th client
a 5th-year senior

Metric Measurement

The meter for length, the gram for weight, and the liter for capacity are the main units of the international metric system. The *American National*

Standard for Metric Practice (1992, pp. 258-292) has a section on the International System of Units and gives rules for usage, rounding, and conversion. Shorter lists may be found in the *Publication Manual of APA* (1994) and in *The Chicago Manual of Style* (1993). *Merriam-Webster's Collegiate Dictionary* (1998) has a list of metric measures and also a table for converting many units of measurement to their metric equivalents.

The journals of the American Psychological Association and many others use the metric system. Refer to the *Publication Manual of APA* for recommended editorial style.

Statistical and Mathematical Material

Manuscript writers decide whether to present statistical and mathematical material in the text or in tables or figures. However, a journal editor may request tables or figures and may also decide against including tables or figures that a writer supplies.

A statistic or a mathematical formula frequently given in journal articles does not require a reference. Statistics and formulas with which many readers are unfamiliar do.

Use Symbols and Abbreviations When Reporting Statistical Material

The symbols for most population statistics, *parameters*, are lowercase Greek letters. Latin letters are used for most of the symbols in sample statistics. In journal articles, symbols are set in standard, **bold**, and *italic* typeface. Use only the standard typeface in your manuscript.

Table 5.1 gives frequently used statistical abbreviations and symbols, including some Greek letters. Writers who do not have the Greek alphabet on their keyboards sometimes write out the letters. Some write out the statistic rather than using the symbol or abbreviation. For a symbol or abbreviation not included in Table 5.1, consult a statistics textbook. Do not rely on a copy editor or a production person to supply a correct one.

Table 5.1. Frequently Used Statistical Abbreviations and Symbols

ANCOVA–analysis of covariance

ANOVA–analysis of variance

d–Cohen's measure of effect size

df–degrees of freedom

f_e–expected frequency

F–Fisher's F ratio

HSD–Tukey's honestly significant difference

K-R 20–Kuder-Richardson formula

LSD–Fisher's least significant difference

M–mean (arithmetic average)

MANOVA–multivariate analysis of variance

Mdn–median

mle–maximum likelihood estimate

mode–most frequently occurring score

MS–mean square

MSE–mean square error

n–number in a subsample

N–number in a sample

ns–nonsignificant

p–probability

P–percentage, percentile

Q–quartile (used also in Cochran's test)

r–Pearson product-moment correlation

r^2 Pearson product-moment correlation squared; coefficient of determination

r_b–biserial correlation

r_s–Spearman rank correlation coefficient

R–multiple correlation; composite rank, a test of significance

R^2–multiple correlation squared; measure of strength of relationship

SD–standard deviation

SE–standard error

SEM–standard error of measurement

SS–sum of squares

t–computed value of t test

Tukey a–Tukey's HSD procedure

x–horizontal axis in a graph

y–vertical axis in a graph

z–standard score

a Alpha; probability of a Type I error; Cronbach's index of internal consistency

ß Beta; probability of a Type II error ($1 - ß$ is statistical power); standardized multiple regression coefficient

g Gamma; Goodman-Kruskal's index of relationship

Δ Delta (cap); increment of change

h^2 Eta squared; measure of strength of relationship

Q Theta (cap); Roy's multivariate criterion

n Nu; degrees of freedom

r_I Rho (with subscript); intraclass correlation coefficient

$\sum$ Sigma (cap); sum or summation

w Phi; measure of association for a contingency table; also a parameter used in determining sample size or statistical power

x^2 Computed value of a chi-square test

When referring to a statistic in the text of a manuscript, write out the term rather than using the symbol. The examples that follow show when to write out a term and when to use a symbol. Recognize that, different from the examples, manuscripts are double-spaced and words are underlined rather than italicized. The right margin is not justified.

Analysis of variance.

Grade 8 students ($M = 60$, $SD = 20$) recalled more than Grade 6 students ($M = 45$, $SD = 20$), $F(1,38) = 26.82$, $MSE = 0.03$, p $<$ .01.

Correlation.

The eight correlations of anxiety with IQ and achievement scores in reading, arithmetic, and language were negative, ranging from - .38 to - .49. All were significant beyond the .01 level. The correlations for girls, - .40, - .38, - .40, and - .43 were consistently lower than the corresponding correlations for boys which were - .47, - .48, - .47, and - .49.

Descriptive statistics.

A comparison of the means showed that the details ($M = 0.62$, $SD = 0.23$) were recalled better than the main ideas ($M = 0.38$, $SD = 0.21$).

Path analysis.

Grades were positively related to standardized achievement test scores (*beta* = .44, p $<$ .001), homework completed (*beta* = .26, p $<$ .001), and attitudes toward school (beta = .15, p $<$ .05).

Chi-square.

The result of the chi-square was significant x^2 (19, $N = 160$) = 28.26, $p <$ .05.

Regression analysis.

Students' academic attitudes in 1988 predicted their 1991 GPAs $F(1,66) = 4.50$, $p <$ .05, $MSE = .64$, $b = .45$, R^2 change = .06.

Use Symbols and Abbreviations When Presenting Mathematical Equations

Some research writing involves giving equations as part of the manuscript. Wherever possible, formulate equations so that they do not extend above or below the line of the text. Use more than two spaces between lines of the text when an equation requires more than one line. Present fractions with the slash (e.g., 1/2, 3/4).

Headings

Researchers use headings to organize their manuscripts. They use from two to five levels of headings, depending on the complexity of the material. Topics of equal importance are given the same level throughout the manuscript. The style for five levels of headings follows:

Level 1 Heading

Centered, Uppercase and Lowercase Main Words

Level 2 Heading

<u>Centered, Underlined, Uppercase and Lowercase Main Words</u>

Level 3 Heading

<u>Flush Left, Underlined, Uppercase and Lowercase Main Words</u>

Level 4 Heading

<u>Paragraph indent, underlined, lowercase.</u>

Level 5 Heading

CENTERED, UPPERCASE ALL LETTERS

The style for entering headings in a manuscript follows. For manuscripts with two levels of headings, use Level 1 and Level 3. For manuscripts with three levels, use Levels 1, 3, and 4. For manuscripts with four levels, use Levels 1, 2, 3, and 4. Use the five levels in a manuscript with five levels but with the Level 5 heading being the main heading, followed with Levels 1, 2, 3, and 4.

Examples of headings from three published projects follow. The first with Level 1 and Level 3 headings is based on one experiment; the second with Levels 1, 3, and 4 headings on a series of ten experiments conducted over a period of two years; the third with Levels 1, 2, 3, and 4 headings on a theory recently formulated. The style of the headings is identical to that for writing a research manuscript. Levels 2, 3, and 4 headings will be italicized in the published article. In the manuscript, different from in the three examples, the title of the publication and the byline should be double-spaced.

Example 1. Research Report With Headings of Two Levels

Problem-solving Behaviors of Children of Low,
Average, and High Intelligence

Herbert J. Klausmeier
University of Wisconsin, Madison

Method

Participants

Problem Solving Tasks

Instructions

Observational Procedure

Data Gathered

Data Analysis

Results

Efficiency of Participants' Problem-Solving Behaviors

Incidence of Nonpersisting Behavior

Incidence of Behavior During Problem Solving

Discussion

References

Note. Nearly every heading in this *Handbook* is Level 1, Level 3, or Level 4. Placement, capitalization, and punctuation of the headings conform to the style recommended in this chapter.

Example 2. Research Report With Headings of Three Levels

Effectiveness of an Instructional Design for
Teaching the Process Concepts of Science

Herbert J. Klausmeier
University of Wisconsin, Madison

Method

Participating Students and Schools

Materials

  Lessons for children.
  Teacher manual.

Instructional Procedure

  Experimental schools.
  Control schools.

Dependent Measures

  Achievement tests.
  Transfer tests.

Data Analysis

Results

Experiments 1-5. First Year

Experiments 6-10. First Year

Experiments 1-5. Second Year

Experiments 6-10. Second Year

Discussion

References

Example 3. Research Report With Headings of Four Levels

A Theory of Concept Learning and Development

Herbert J. Klausmeier
University of Wisconsin, Madison

Four Levels of Conceptual Understanding

Mental Operations Involved in Learning Concepts at
Successively Higher Levels of Understanding

Attending and Discriminating

Concrete Level

Identity and Classificatory Levels

Formal Level

Remembering Stimulus Information

Memory at the Concrete Level

Memory at the Identity and Classificatory Levels

Memory at the Formal Level

Generalizing and Higher-Order Operations

Generalizing Equivalence at the Classificatory Level

Higher Operations at the Formal Level

Discriminating the attributes.
Inferring the concept from common attributes of examples.
Inferring the concept by testing hypotheses.
Remembering hypotheses and stimulus information.
Evaluating hypotheses to ascertain the concept.

The Role of Language in Facilitating Concept Attainment

Applications of the Theory

Discussion

References

Quotations

A direct quotation includes exactly what an author said or wrote (e.g., The therapist said, "I will continue," and she did.). An indirect quotation gives the substance but changes the wording to fit the context as in the following: The therapist said that she would continue and she did.

When preparing a manuscript, enclose a direct quotation of fewer than 40 words in double quotation marks (see Chapter 4 for using double quotation marks both with and without other punctuation). Enclose in single quotation marks anything that was enclosed originally in double quotation marks as follows: "The therapist reported that a 'heart palpitation of 190' led to the patient's panic."

Reproducing Quoted Material

When reproducing material from a published source, give the wording, spelling, and punctuation exactly as in the source. Put a quotation of fewer than 40 words in the text of the manuscript and enclose it in double quotation marks. Indent the lines of longer quotations five spaces, double-space the material, but *do not* enclose the block of typed lines in quotation marks. The following examples reflect these points and also show minor changes that a writer can make when reproducing quoted material.

Example: Fewer Than 40 Words and Two Minor Changes

Klausmeier and Allen (1978) concluded: "We found that the vast majority of students acquired the *successively higher levels of the same concepts* [italics added] in an invariant sequence." (p. 269). The authors then explained the invariant sequence that emerged across the school years as a product of learning and mental maturation.

The preceding example shows how to proceed with a direct quotation of fewer than 40 words. It also shows two minor changes that may be made in a direct quotation. First, the first letter of the first quoted word was changed from lowercase to uppercase. A first letter can also be changed from uppercase to lowercase. Second, to indicate emphasis, the seven words were italicized and [italics added] was entered.

Example: More Than 40 Words and a Minor Change

Klausmeier, Wiersma, and Harris (1963) carried out an experiment on concept identification. They invented the concepts to be learned rather than using real-world concepts. In the experiment, each participant, after a short introduction to the experimenter, received the following instructions:

> This experiment is concerned with how people attain concepts. You are going to have an opportunity to attain several concepts. You will be shown a display of cards with various borders, figures, and colors. (The participant was then shown a 32-card display board. The two defining characteristics of each attribute were pointed out, i.e., one or two figures, large or small figures, red or green figures, and circular or elliptical figures.) . . . Can you show me what cards on this display board . . . (p. 162).

This 1963 quotation indicates how to handle quotations of 40 words or longer. It also shows how a change can be made (i.e., entering ellipsis points to indicate that part of the quotation is omitted).

Crediting Sources and Securing Permission

Publishers require a writer to credit the source of paraphrased material and direct quotations. The two prior examples show how to give credit.

Publishers typically ask writers to secure permission to reproduce figures, tables, and text material of 500 words or more. However, there is variation among publishers related to the 500 words. Editors inform writers regarding the requirements and often supply forms for securing permissions.

Chapter 6

FOOTNOTES, NOTES, TABLES, AND FIGURES

Manuscript authors use footnotes and notes to supplement material provided in the text. They use tables and figures to present information more concisely than can be done in written form. As will be seen, the style requirements for tables and figures are much more detailed than for footnotes and notes.

Footnotes and Notes

Two kinds of footnotes may be used in the text: content and permission. There are two kinds of notes: author and table.

Footnotes

Content footnotes supplement and amplify material in the text. Writers should limit the use of content footnotes. Essential footnotes should be kept short. A footnote that might be longer than a sentence or two should be worked into the text or placed in an appendix.

Permission footnotes are required for reproducing material that is copyrighted. It is the author's responsibility to determine when permission is required.

Author Note

Authors provide information about themselves and their work in a note that appears on the first page of the printed article. The note is typed, double-spaced.

The first paragraph of the note as is shown in Exhibit 6.1 gives the names of the authors and their university affiliations. Authors not affiliated with a university or other organization provide the names of their city and state.

Authors not in the United States give their city and country. If an article is by one author, the first paragraph is not needed because the same information is given in the mailing address at the end of the third paragraph.

The second paragraph of the author note as is shown in Exhibit 6.1 acknowledges financial support and personal assistance. There is a disclaimer, indicating that the article does not necessarily reflect the views of the funding agency. The second paragraph of a different author note might have supplied other information, such as the article being based on a doctoral dissertation or on a presidential address.

The third paragraph supplies a complete mailing address of the first author. A different author might have ended the paragraph with an address for e-mail.

Numbering and Submitting Footnotes and Notes

Number content and permission footnotes consecutively throughout a manuscript. Do not number the author note.

Exhibit 6.1. Example of an Author Note

Herbert J. Klausmeier, University of Wisconsin; William Wiersma, University of Toledo; and Chester W. Harris, University of California, Santa Barbara.

This research was supported by the U.S. Office of Educational Research and Improvement. The views expressed do not necessarily reflect those of the supporting organization. We wish to thank Thomas Sipple for his assistance in gathering the research data.

Correspondence concerning this article should be addressed to Herbert J. Klausmeier, Department of Educational Psychology, 1025 W. Johnson Street, Madison, WI 53706.

Start the author note on a separate page and also the numbered footnotes on a separate page. When submitting a manuscript, place the author page immediately preceding the footnote page(s). Place the author and footnote pages immediately after the appendix, if there is one, or after the reference list and immediately preceding the tables.

Tables

Tables enable authors to present a large amount of information in a small amount of space. A half-page table can give detailed statistical information that would require pages of text. Moreover, the table information might be more easily understood and remembered.

Tables must incorporate an increasingly wide variety of statistical analyses. This poses a problem for some researchers. However, options are available to solve the problem. Often researchers can locate articles in which there are tables that present statistical analyses identical to theirs. Another option is to get needed information from the editor of the journal to which a manuscript will be submitted. A third option is to refer to *Presenting Your Findings: A Practical Guide for Creating Tables* (Nicol & Pexman, 1999). The book provides examples of tables with many different statistical analyses. Manuscript authors will probably be able to locate an example for any statistic they use.

It is beyond the scope of this *Handbook* to provide examples of tables. Instead, information relevant for preparing tables in general follows.

Title

The title of a table should clearly indicate the substance of the table. In composing table titles, try to ensure that they are not too short, thereby not conveying the needed information, nor too long, giving unnecessary details.

Headings

Headings show how the information in the body of a table is organized and the kind of information in the column(s) below the headings. All columns of information must have headings. Usually the independent variables are listed in the left column of the table.

Use standard abbreviations and symbols in the headings. Explain abbreviations of specific terms in a table note.

Table Ruling

Horizontal lines, called rules, are preferred in tables; vertical rules are rarely accepted. When preparing a table, extend a rule across the width of the table immediately below the title of the table, above the columns of data, and below the body of the table. A rule extending across the table may be placed between the main parts of a table, or the parts may be separated by increasing the blank space between the parts.

Shorter rules are placed below the individual column heads. Inasmuch as the column heads are centered above the respective columns, placing the rules beneath the heads contributes esthetically to the appearance of a table.

Table Notes

Table notes are general, specific, or probability. A general note, indicated by *Note*, clarifies information that relates to the table in its entirety. A specific note, indicated by a superscript lowercase letter, refers to the information in a column, row, or to an individual entry. A probability note, indicated by one or more asterisks, refers to tests of significance, the fewer the asterisks the lesser the level of significance (e.g., $*p < .05$, $**p < .01$, $***p < .001$.).

Notes are placed below the table in this order: general, specific, probability. Start each note flush with the left margin of the table and double space the note. Enter the word *Note* only for the general note.

Citing and Numbering Tables

A table appears in a printed article as close as possible to its citation in the text. However, the table does not precede the citation unless it appears on the same page as the citation. To indicate desired placement, write out *Table* in the margin of the page on the line where it is first cited in the text and enter the table number (e.g., Table 1, Table 2, and so on). A production person will place the tables in the article.

Number tables consecutively in the manuscript. If an appendix has tables, number them consecutively with the appendix designation and the table number (e.g., Table A1, Table A2, and so on).

Explaining Table Information in the Text

After citing a table, explain any concept that may not be understood by journal readers. Indicate highlights to be examined. Write out a conclusion that readers should draw but might miss. Do not duplicate detailed table information.

Submitting Tables

Submit the tables on white bond paper. Order the tables according to the table numbers. In the transmittal package, place the group of tables immediately after the set of footnotes.

Figures

Four kinds of figures commonly found in journals are graphs, charts, drawings, and photographs. Figures make complex subject matter more quickly and more easily understood. They capture the essence of the material.

The quantitative information in figures is typically not as exact as that in tables. The reader estimates and gets an approximation of the exact values.

Whether or not to prepare a figure requires careful consideration. Some writers may not have the tools or the skills to prepare the sophisticated artwork that the particular ideas demand. Getting the figure properly placed in a manuscript may present a problem.

Preparing figures and getting them published requires considerable effort by the manuscript author and the production staff of the journal. Accordingly, it is advisable to prepare only those figures that markedly lessen the amount of information required in the text and that substantially increase comprehension and interest.

Guides to follow relative to figures in general are:
- Choose a graph, chart, or drawing that presents the desired information most concisely and clearly.
- Keep the figure simple, easily readable, and free of extraneous material.
- Plot the data accurately in a format that can be understood readily.
- Explain the abbreviations and symbols in the figure caption or the figure legend so that the text does not have to be consulted to get the message of the figure.
- Mention every figure in the text.
- Provide written permission for figures that are reproduced from another source.

Graphs

Graphs show relationships in sets of information. Some relationships can be made more comprehensible in a graph than in words in the text, for example, in a scatter graph showing the pattern of scores for a correlation.

Line graphs. Line graphs show relationships between two quantitative variables. The dependent variable is listed on the vertical axis of the graph, the independent variable on the horizontal axis. Dots or other small marks that represent individual scores or other scores, such as means, are entered and a line connecting the marks is drawn.

Bar graphs. Bar graphs indicate relationships between an independent variable that is categorical (e.g., kinds of leadership) and a continuous dependent variable (e.g., percent of time spent in activity). The bars may be horizontal or vertical. Both the number of categorical variables and the number of variables within each category may vary.

Circle graphs. Circle graphs clarify relationships involving proportions and percentages. The segments of a circle graph are presented clockwise, starting at 12 o'clock. The sequence in presenting the segments is from largest to smallest. The segments may be kept clear or they may be shaded from lighter to darker.

Scatter graphs. With a small number of participants, a dot or other small mark representing the values of each participant's two performances can be plotted to produce a scatter graph. With larger numbers of participants, the number of participants having identical performance measures may be plotted. The resulting pattern of the plot implies a correlation between the two performance measures.

A scatter graph may help a reader estimate the importance of a correlation. Some readers attach too much importance to a low but statistically significant correlation. Other readers may not recognize how scores vary when a correlation is high.

Charts

Charts are of three main kinds: flow charts, organizational charts, and schematics. Flow charts reflect the sequence of elements of a process (e.g., developing an understanding of concepts during the school years). The process may be of shorter or longer duration and the elements may be few to many. Organizational charts show the relationship among elements of a group or an organization (e.g., three hierarchical decision-making groups in a school district). A schematic indicates the components of a system (e.g., a nonconventional system of schooling).

Drawings

Drawings may be used to display any element of a research study that is not entirely verbal or quantitative. For example, it may be instructive to use a drawing to show a piece of experimental equipment or a test item.

Researchers have considerable freedom to incorporate in a drawing whatever will enhance clarity and meaningfulness. However, an artist may be needed to prepare an acceptable drawing.

Photographs

Photographs stimulate interest as well as provide information. Some publishers regularly insert a photograph of the author(s) in the journal article.

Except in unusual cases, photographs should be in black-and-white film. Color photography is more expensive and more difficult to reproduce than black and white. If it is necessary to show something in color, consult the journal editor.

A photograph is usually better when any part of it not to be reproduced is eliminated, that is, cropped. When cropped, the print should have straight vertical and horizontal lines. Cropping may change the shape of the figure; this presents no problem to production personnel.

If people are photographed, get their signed permission to publish the photograph. If a photograph is from another source, secure permission to publish it and acknowledge the copyright holder and the author in the caption of the figure.

Figure Captions and Legends

A caption serves as the title of a figure. In the printed article, it appears below the figure. However, when figures are submitted with a manuscript, the captions are not placed on the figures. Instead, type all figure captions, starting on a separate sheet of paper, and submit them with the manuscript.

A legend is part of the figure, not part of the caption. Accordingly, it is prepared and submitted as an integral element of the figure. A legend requires the same kind of lettering and also the identical proportion of length and width as the rest of the figure. If an element of a legend cannot be made readily comprehensible, clarifying information should be put in the caption, immediately following the first descriptive information.

Size and Proportion of Figures

Figures must be of the correct size and proportion to fit a journal's page. The pages of journals vary in size (e.g., 6 x 9 in., 8 x 11 in.). Journals with large pages (e.g., 8 x 11 in.) may have two or more columns. Accordingly, one important aspect of figure preparation is to identify the journal to which the manuscript and the figures will be sent. Then prepare figures that can be reproduced as submitted or that can be reduced in size and yet be of the desired proportion. The figure includes the material in the legend so any typed material must also be of the proper size and proportion.

Detailed suggestions for preparing figures so that their size and proportion will fit the specifications of particular journals is beyond the scope of this *Handbook.* To secure the specifications, consult the journal editor.

Citing and Numbering Figures

Production personnel place a figure as close as possible to its first citation in the text, but not preceding the citation unless the figure appears on the same page as the citation. Mark your manuscript (e.g., Figure 1, Figure 2, etc.) on the line where the figure is first cited to indicate the desired location. Number the figures consecutively throughout the manuscript.

Handling Completed Figures

Figures will appear in an article exactly as they have been submitted, except that they may be reduced or increased in size. Accordingly, exercise care in handling them. Do not use staples or paper clips to attach anything to a figure. Scratches and indentations cannot be eliminated. Use a soft pencil to give the number of the figure and the title of the manuscript on the back side of the figure. A self-sticking tape that will in no way mar the figure is another option.

Submitting Figures and Captions

Submit the figures in numerical order, starting with a separate page. Placing each figure on a sheet of white paper is acceptable for the first draft of the manuscript. For the final draft, place each figure on a high-quality, bright, white sheet of paper or photograph it and submit it as an 8 x 10 glossy print.

Submit the captions in numerical order, starting with a separate page. Place the set of captions immediately after the group of tables and preceding the set of figures.

Chapter 7

REFERENCE CITATIONS IN THE TEXT AND REFERENCES IN THE REFERENCE LIST

Researchers document their sources of information by citing the author and date of each source in the text. The citations in the text enable the reader to locate the sources in the alphabetical reference list at the end of the article. Accordingly, research writing calls for accuracy of the citations in the text and accuracy and completeness of the references in the reference list.

Reference Citations in the Text

The guides and examples that follow give the style for variations in the number of authors and in the kind of authorship. The first guide is followed with examples showing three different ways of citing a given reference. To save space and undue repetition, later guides have only one or two examples.

One Author

Include the year after the author's surname the first time one author is cited in a paragraph. In the same paragraph where one author is cited, give only the surname, not the year, except if not giving the year results in confusion with some other citation.

Klausmeier (1996) reported that gifted second-grade children experienced no negative effects from being accelerated to the fourth grade.

No negative effects of accelerating . . . were reported (Klausmeier, 1996).

In 1996, Klausmeier reported no negative effects . . .

Two Authors

Cite the surnames of both authors throughout the manuscript. (Notice the use of and and & in the examples.)

Klausmeier and Allen (1978) found that the concept attainment of some high-achieving third-grade children was as high as that of some low-achieving high school seniors.

The concept attainment of some high-achieving third-grade children was found . . . (Klausmeier & Allen, 1978).

Three, Four, or Five Authors

Give the surnames of all three, four, or five authors in the first citation in a paragraph; thereafter, in the same paragraph give the surname of only the first author and follow it with et al. Do not underline et al. When citing the source in later paragraphs the first time, enter the surname of the first author and follow it with et al. and the year.

Deater-Deckard, Scarr, McCartney, and Eisenberg (1994) reported . . . [first citation]

Deater-Deckard et al. reported . . . [second and later citations in the same paragraph]

Deater-Deckard et al. (1994) reported . . . [first citation in later paragraphs]

Six or More Authors

In the first and later citations, cite only the surname of the first of six or more authors followed by et al. Cite the surnames of the first authors and as many subsequent authors as needed to distinguish two references by six or more authors.

Arnold, et al. (1972)

Coleman, Campbell, Hobson, et al. (1966)

Coleman, Campbell, Jones, et al. (1966)

Groups as Authors

Associations, corporations, government agencies, study groups, and so on are authors of articles, books, manuals, and other publications. When citing a group author, spell out its name the first time it is cited. Thereafter, if the name is long, abbreviate it. Do not abbreviate a short name or any name that would cause uncertainty or confusion.

First citation. (American Educational Research Association [AERA], 1994); thereafter, (AERA, 1994)

First citation. (University of Nevada, 1998); thereafter, (University of Nevada, 1998); not (UN, 1998)

No Author

Cite the first few words of the reference as entered in the reference list. Use quotation marks to indicate a chapter or an article. Underline the title of a book, brochure, periodical, or report. The title will be in italics when the manuscript is published.

Task 4 presents ("Stage theory, 1968")

a booklet, *Research on Gender* (1987)

Anonymous Work

Put the word *Anonymous* in the text; give the publication date.

Two Authors With the Same Surname

When two or more authors with the same surname are listed in the reference list, place the first author's initials in all of the text citations.

C. W. Harris (1971) and M. L. Harris (1972) outlined . . .

M. L. Harris and Romberg (1971) and M. L. Harris and Voelker (1971) analyzed . . .

Two or More Publications by Different Authors (Enclosed in parentheses)

Enter the surnames in alphabetical order; separate the citations by semi-colons.

> Two studies (Nichols, in press; Sandoval, Frisby, Geisinger, Ramos-Grenier, & Scheuneman, 1998) reported their . . .

Two or More Publications by the Same Author(s) Having the Same Publication Date (Enclosed in parentheses)

Give the surname(s) once; follow the year with a, b, c, and so on.

> Conceptual development progressed . . . (Klausmeier, 1985a, 1985b)

Two or More Publications in Different Years by the Same Author(s) (Enclosed in parentheses)

Give the surname(s) once. Enter the year or in press after the surname(s) in the order of publications; in press last.

> The effects of focused instruction . . . (Klausmeier, 1971, 1996, in press)

Parts of a Source

Indicate the page(s), figure, table, or other item after the year. Abbreviate *pages* and *chapter*.

> (Klausmeier, 1996, pp. 99-115)

> (Klausmeier & Allen, 1978, chap. 1)

Personal Communications

Cite unpublished letters, memoranda, telephone conversations, E-mail, and other kinds of nonrecoverable electronic communications in the text. Do not include personal communications in the reference list because they cannot be recovered. (In the example, notice that the author's initial is given and also the exact date of the communication.)

> (B. Underwood, personal communication, April 13, 1972)

References in the Reference List

Journal articles that report research have reference lists. Sources cited in the text, except unpublished communications, must have corresponding entries in the reference list. There must be no reference in the reference list that is not cited in the text. Each entry in the list must be correct and complete. (References included in a meta-analysis are integrated into the reference list and are identified with an asterisk that precedes the reference.)

Careful selection of references improves the prospect of getting a manuscript published. Do not include any reference that is obsolescent, is of little significance, is weak with respect to the method, or has trivial conclusions. If a study, though excellent in all other respects, contributes little knowledge to the field, consider not including it.

Abbreviation of Terms

Some words in the entries of the reference list must be abbreviated. Exhibit 7.1 gives abbreviations in nonlegal references, in legal references, and for the states and territories.

Location of Publishers

Give the names of major U.S. cities but not the names of the states. Give the names of major cities outside the United States but not the countries.

Major Cities

Baltimore	Amsterdam
Boston	Jerusalem
Chicago	London
Los Angeles	Milan
New York	Moscow
Philadelphia	Paris
San Francisco	Rome
	Stockholm
	Tokyo
	Vienna

Exhibit 7.1. Abbreviations in Nonlegal References, in Legal References, and for the States and Territories

Nonlegal References

chap.	chapter
ed.	edition
Rev. ed.	revised edition
2nd ed.	second edition
Ed. (Eds.)	Editor (Editors)
Trans.	Translator(s)
n.d.	no date
p. (pp.)	page (pages)
Vol.	Volume (as in Vol. 4)
vols.	volumes (as in 4 vols.)
No.	Number
Pt.	Part
Tech.Rep.	Technical Report
Suppl.	Supplement

Legal References

Cong.	U.S. Congress
H.R.	House of Representatives
S.	Senate
Reg.	Regulation
Res.	Resolution
F.	*Federal Reporter*
F.2d	*Federal Reporter, Second Series*
F. Supp.	*Federal Supplement*
U.S.C.	*United States Code*
Stat.	*United States Statutes at Large*
U.S.C.A.	*United States Code Annotated*
U.S.	*United States Reports*
S.Ct.	*Supreme Court Reporter*
Fed. Reg.	*Federal Register*
Cong. Rec.	*Congressional Record*

States and Territories

AL	Alabama	MO	Missouri
AK	Alaska	MT	Montana
AS	American Samoa	NE	Nebraska
AZ	Arizona	NV	Nevada
AR	Arkansas	NH	New Hampshire
CA	California	NJ	New Jersey
CZ	Canal Zone	NM	New Mexico
CO	Colorado	NY	New York
CT	Connecticut	NC	North Carolina
DE	Delaware	ND	North Dakota
DC	District of Columbia	OH	Ohio
FL	Florida	OK	Oklahoma
GA	Georgia	OR	Oregon
GU	Guam	PA	Pennsylvania
HI	Hawaii	PR	Puerto Rico
ID	Idaho	RI	Rhode Island
IL	Illinois	SC	South Carolina
IN	Indiana	SD	South Dakota
IA	Iowa	TN	Tennessee
KS	Kansas	TX	Texas
KY	Kentucky	UT	Utah
LA	Louisiana	VT	Vermont
ME	Maine	VA	Virginia
MD	Maryland	VI	Virgin Islands
MA	Massachusetts	WA	Washington
MI	Michigan	WV	West Virginia
MN	Minnesota	WI	Wisconsin
MS	Mississippi	WY	Wyoming

Articles in Journals, Magazines, Newsletters, Newspapers, Special Issues of Journals, and Journals Published Annually

The style for the author part of references in the reference list is identical for journals, books, and all other publications. The next part of this chapter has examples of references for journal articles with all author variations: no author, one author, two authors, three authors, four authors, five authors, and six or more authors. Examples are given of only some of the author variations for the publications that come after the journal articles. If an author pattern not given for a later publication is needed, refer back to the journal example.

Journal article, no author.

Instructions in regard to preparation of a manuscript. (1929). *Psychological Bulletin, 26,* 57-63.

Journal article, one author.

Klausmeier, H. J. (1992). Concept learning and concept teaching. *Educational Psychologist, 27,* 267-286.

Journal article, two authors.

Wilt, S., & Olson, S. (1996). Prevalence of domestic violence in the United States. *Journal of American Medical Women's Association, 51,* 77-82.

Journal article, three, four, or five authors.

Woodall, W. G., Davis, D. K., & Sahin, H. (1983). From the boob tube to the black box: Television news comprehension from an information processing perspective. *Journal of Broadcasting, 27,* 1-23.

Deater-Deckard, K., Scarr, S., McCartney, K., & Eisenberg, J. (1994). Paternal separation anxiety: Relationships with parenting stress, child-rearing attitudes, and maternal anxieties. *Psychological Science, 5*(6), 341-346.

MacMillan, H. L., MacMillan, J. H., Offord, D. R., Griffith, L., & MacMillan, A. (1994). Primary prevention of child abuse and neglect: A critical review. Part I. *Journal of Child Psychology, Psychiatry, and Allied Disciplines, 35,* 835-856.

Journal article, six or more authors.

Eccles, J. S., Wigfield, A., Midgley, C., Reuman, D., MacIver, D., & Feldlaufer, H. (1993). Negative effects of traditional middle schools on students' motivation. *Elementary School Journal, 93,* 553-574.

Journal article, non-English, translated into English.

Boron, A. A. (1981). La crisis Norteamericana y la racionalidad neoconsservadora [The U. S. crisis and neoconservative rationality]. *CIDE Cuadernos Semestrales, 9,* 31-38.

Journal article, in press.

> Nichols, J. D. (in press). The effects of cooperative learning on student achievement and motivation in a high school geometry class. *Contemporary Educational Psychology.*

Journal article, reply to other authors.

> Jacobson, N. S., Gottman, J. M., & Shortt, J. W. (1995). The distinction between Type 1 and Type 2 batterers–further considerations: Reply to Ordnuff et al. (1995), Margolin et al.(1995), and Walker (1995), *Journal of Family Psychology, 9,* 272-279.

Journal article, supplement.

> Wolfe, D. A., Reppucci, N. D., & Hart, S. (1995). Child abuse prevention: Knowledge and priorities. *Journal of Clinical Child Psychology, 24* (Suppl.), 5-23.

Magazine article.

> Merkin, D. (1998, November 9). Freud rising. *New Yorker,* 50-55.

Magazine article, Jr. in author's name.

> Apple, R. W., Jr. (1998, November 15). Hollywood, D.C. *New York Times Magazine,* 40, 42, 44.

Newsletter article, no author.

> Science shines in San Francisco. (1998, November/December). *Psychological Science Agenda, 11,* 8, 18-19.

Newsletter article, one author.

> Parasuraman, R. (1998, November/December). Probing the attentive brain at work and in disease. *Psychological Science Agenda,* 6-8.

Daily newspaper article, no author.

> Typhus's gene makeup unlocked. (1998, November 18). *The San Diego Union-Tribune,* p. E12.

Daily newspaper article, discontinuous pages.

Goode, E. (1998, November 3). New hope for loser in the battle to stay awake. *The New York Times*, pp. D1, 8.

Monthly newspaper article, one author.

McIntosh, H. (1998, November). Neuroimaging tools offer new ways to study autism. *APA Monitor*, p. 15.

Monthly newspaper article, letter to editor.

Gianotti, P. (1998, November). Worthy of honor? [Letter to editor]. *APA Monitor*, pp. 5-6.

Journal, special issue.

Hetherington, E. M. (Ed.). (1998). Applications of developmental science. [Special issue]. *American Psychologist, 89*(1).

Journal published annually.

Scarr, S., & Eisenberg, M. (1993). Child care research: Issues, perspectives, and results. *Annual Review of Psychology, 44*, 613-644.

Monographs and Abstracts

Monograph, with issue number and serial number.

Hetherington, E.M., & Clingempeel, W. G. (1992). Coping with marital transitions: A family systems perspective. *Monographs of the Society for Research in Child Development, 57* (2-3, Serial No. 227).

Monograph, bound into a journal.

Ganster, D. C., Schaubroeck, J., Sime, W. E., & Mayes, B. T. (1991). The homological validity of the Type A personality among employed adults [Monograph]. *Journal of Applied Psychology, 76*, 143-168.

Abstract, original source.

Woolf, N. J., Young, S. L., Fanselow, M. S., & Butcher, L. L. (1991). MAP-2 expression in cholinoceptive pyramidal cells of rodent cortex and hippocampus is altered by Pavlovian conditioning. *Society for Neuroscience Abstracts, 17*, 480.

Abstract, secondary source.

Nakazato, K., Shimonaka, Y., & Homma, A. (1992). Cognitive functions of centenarians: The Tokyo Metropolitan Centenarian Study. *Japanese Journal of Developmental Psychology, 3*, 9-16. (From *PsychSCAN: Neuropsychology*, 1993, 2, Abstract No. 604).

Books, Booklets, Manuals, and Book Supplements – Varying Author - ship

Book, no author or editor.

The bluebook. A uniform system of citation (15th ed.). (1991). Cambridge, MA: Harvard Law Review Association.

Book, dictionary.

Merriam-Webster's collegiate dictionary (10th ed.). (1998). Springfield, MA: Merriam-Webster.

Book, one author.

Klausmeier, H. J. (1985). *Educational psychology* (5th ed.). New York: Harper & Row.

Book, two authors.

Klausmeier, H. J., & Allen, P. S. (1978). *Cognitive development of children and youth: A longitudinal study.* New York: Academic Press.

Book, three to five authors.

Clarke-Stewart, K. A., Gruber, C. P., & Fitzgerald, L. M. (1994). *Children at home and in day care.* Hillsdale, NJ: Erlbaum.

Book, six or more authors.

Coleman, J., Campbell, E., Hobson, C., McPartland, J., Mood, A., Weinfield, J., & York, R. (1966). *Equality of educational opportunity.* Washington, DC: U. S. Government Printing Office.

Book, group author, government agency.

Department of Justice. (1992). *Sourcebook of criminal justice statistics, 1991.* Washington, DC: U.S. Government Printing Office.

Book, group author, private agency.

Carnegie Task Force on Teaching as a Profession. (1986). *A nation prepared: Teachers for the 21st century.* New York: Carnegie Forum on Education and the Economy.

Book, English translation.

Piaget, J. (1971). *Psychology and epistemology: Towards a theory of knowledge.* (A. Rosin, Trans.). New York: Viking Press.

Book, non-English.

Skaalvik, S. (1995). *Voksne med lese–og skrivevansker forteller om sine skoleerfaringer* [School experiences among adults with reading and writing problems]. Trondheim, Norway: norsk voksenpedagogisk institutt.

Book, republished.

Riesman, D. (1969). *The lonely crowd.* New Haven, CT: Yale University Press. [Original work published 1950].

Booklet.

Center for a Woman's Own Name. (1974). *Booklet for women who wish to determine their own names after marriage.* Barrington, IL: Author.

Manual.

Jacobson, J. W., & Mulick, J. A. (Eds.). (1996). *Manual of diagnosis and professional practice in mental retardation.* Washington, DC: American Psychological Association.

Book supplement.

Garmezy, N. (1985). Stress-resistant children: The search for protective factors. In J. E. Stevenson (Ed.), *Recent research in developmental psychopathology: Journal of Child Psychology and Psychiatry Book Supplement 4* (pp. 213-233). Oxford: Pergamon Press.

Books, Book Articles, and Book Chapters – Varying Editorship

Book, one editor.

Morris, J. A. (Ed.). (1997). *Practicing psychology in rural areas: Hospital privileges and collaborative care.* Washington, DC: American Psychological Association.

Book, two editors.

Pressman, M. R., & Orr, W. C. (Eds.). (1997). *Understanding sleep: The evaluation and treatment of sleep disorders.* Washington, DC: American Psychological Association.

Book, three to five editors.

Sandoval, J., Frisby, C., Geisinger, K., Ramos-Grenier, J., & Scheuneman, J. (Eds.). (1998). *Test interpretation and diversity: Achieving equity in assessment.* Washington, DC: American Psychological Association.

Book article, in encyclopedia.

Klausmeier, H. J. (1978). Concept learning. In R. J. Corsini (Ed.), *Concise encyclopedia of psychology* (pp. 231-233). New York: Wiley.

Book chapter, one author, two editors.

Klausmeier, H. J. (1996). The role of the researcher in educational improvement: A retrospective analysis. In C. B. Benbow & D. Lubinski (Eds.), *Intellectual talent: Psychometric and social issues* (pp. 99-115). Baltimore, MD: The Johns Hopkins University Press.

Book chapter, two authors, two editors.

> Byrne, D., & Murnen, S. (1988). Maintaining loving relationships. In R. Sternberg & M. Barnes (Eds.), *The psychology of love* (pp. 293-310). New Haven: Yale University Press.

Book chapter, two authors, a series editor, a volume editor, with volume number and book edition given.

> Ruble, D. N., & Martin, N. (1998). Gender. In W. Damon (Series Ed.) & N. Eisenberg (Vol. Ed.), *Handbook of child psychology* (Vol. 3, 5th ed.). New York: Wiley.

Book chapter, group author, one editor.

> Santa Barbara Classroom Discourse Group. (1992). Constructing literacy in classrooms: Literate action as social accomplishment. In H. H. Marshall (Ed.), *Redefining student learning: Roots of educational change* (pp. 119-150). Norwood, NJ: Ablex.

Research and Technical Reports

Report, available from Educational Resource Information Center (ERIC).

> Klausmeier, H. J., Hooper, F. H., & Sipple, T. S. (1976). *A preliminary report of the relationship between Piaget's and Klausmeier's measures of children's cognitive development* (Tech. Rep. No. 426). Madison: University of Wisconsin, Wisconsin Center for Education Research. (ERIC Document Reproduction Service No. 154-006).

Report, available from National Technical Information Service (NTIS).

> Osgood, D. W., & Wilson, J. K. (1990). *Covariation of adolescent health problems.* Lincoln: University of Nebraska. (NTIS No. PB 91-154 377/AS).

Report, available from Government Printing Office.

> U.S. Department of Health and Human Services, National Center on Child Abuse and Neglect. (1997). *Child maltreatment 1995: Reports*

from the states to the National Center on Child Abuse and Neglect. Washington, DC: U.S. Government Printing Office.

Report, available from U. S. government agency, not GPO.

Ventura, S. J., Martin, J. A., Curtin, S. C., & Mathews, T. J. (1997). Report of final natality statistics, 1995. *Monthly Vital Statistics Report, 45* (11, Suppl. 2). Hyattsville, MD: National Center for Health Statistics.

Report, available from private source.

Gallup, G. H., Moore, D. W., & Schussel, R. (1995). *Disciplining children in America: A Gallup Poll Report.* Princeton, NJ: The Gallup Organization.

Technical report, available from university.

Klausmeier, H. J. (1963). *Results of experimentation with acceleration of elementary school students and team teaching, Racine, Wisconsin* (Tech. Rep. No. 63-8). Madison, WI: University of Wisconsin, School of Education.

Working paper, available from university.

Hallinan, M. (1976). *Friendship formation: A continuous time Markov process* (CD Working Paper 86-5). Madison: University of Wisconsin Center for Demography and Ecology.

Papers and Symposium Contributions

Lecture, unpublished, presented at an annual meeting.

Klerman, L. V. (1993, March). *Adolescent pregnancy and parenting: Controversies of the past and lessons for the future.* Gallagher Lecture presented at the annual meeting of the Society for Adolescent Medicine, Chicago.

Lecture, unpublished, available from a university.

Klausmeier, H. J. (1972). *Individually Guided Education: An alternative system of elementary schooling.* (Harlan E. Anderson Lecture). New Haven, CT: Yale University, Institution for Social and Policy Studies.

Paper, unpublished, presented at a national meeting in U. S.

Baumert, J. (1995, April). *Gender, science interest, teaching strategies and socially shared beliefs about gender roles in 7th graders–A multi-level analysis.* Paper presented at the annual meeting of the American Educational Research Association, San Francisco.

Paper, unpublished, presented at a conference.

Hidi, S., & Berndorff, D. (1996, June). *Situational interest and learning.* Paper presented at the Seeon Conference on Gender and Interest, Kloster, Seeon, Germany.

Paper, unpublished, presented at an international meeting.

Klausmeier, H. J. (1985). *Effects of schooling on students' educational development.* Paper presented at the *XX* Interamerican Congress of Psychology, Caracas, Venezuela.

Symposium contribution, published in edited book.

Eccles, J. S. (1984). Sex differences in achievement patterns. In T. Sonderegger (Ed.), *Nebraska Symposium on Motivation* (Vol. 32, pp. 97-132). Lincoln: University of Nebraska Press.

Symposium contribution, published in symposium proceedings.

Klausmeier, H. J. (1979). Experience and cognitive development. *In Proceedings of the International Symposium on Physics, Biology, and Mathematics: Different Approaches in an Integrated Curriculum for the Primary School* (pp. 33-71). Rome: Italian Academy of Science.

Manuscripts

Manuscript, submitted for publication.

Manger, T., & Eikeland, O. J. (1996). *Gender differences in self-perceived mathematics competence and motivation.* Manuscript submitted for publication, University of Bergen, Norway.

Manuscript, unpublished.

Huizinga, D., Esbensen, F.A., & Weiher, A. (1996). The impact of arrest on subsequent delinquent behavior. In R. Loeber, D. Huizinga, & T. Thornberry (Eds.), *Program of Research on the Causes and Correlates of Delinquency Annual Report 1995-1996.* Unpublished manuscript.

Reviews

Review, book.

Klausmeier, H. J. (1968). Essential or helpful [Review of the book *Essentials of learning: An overview for students of education.* 2nd ed.]. *Contemporary Psychology, 13,* 574.

Review, film.

Kauffmann, S. (1989, October 9). Turbulent lives. [Review of the film *A dry white season*]. *New Republic,* 24, 25.

Published Tests

Test, achievement.

Dunn, D. D., & Markwardt, F. (1988). *Peabody Individual Achievement Test–Revised.* Circle Pines, MN: American Guidance Service.

Test, intelligence.

Wechsler, D. (1998). *Wechsler Adult Intelligence Scale–III* (3rd ed.). New York: Psychological Corporation.

Audiovisual Media

Cassette recording, music.

Marsalis, B. (1986). *Romances for saxophone* [Cassette]. New York: CBS.

Cassette recording, speaker.

Klausmeier, H. J. (1991). *Concept learning and concept teaching.* (Cassette Recording No. 91-033). Washington, DC: American Psychological Association.

Cassette recording, video.

Sylvester, R. (1998, November). *On social interaction and brain development.* [Video]. Bloomington, IN: Phi Delta Kappa.

Film.

Capra, F. (Director). (1946). *It's a wonderful life.* [Film]. RKO.

Television broadcast.

Crystal, L. (Executive Producer). (1998, December 7). *The news hour with Jim Lehrer.* New York and Washington, DC: Public Broadcasting Service.

Television, series.

Lindsey, L., & Shulberg, S. (Vice-Presidents). (1996). *American playhouse.* New York: WNET.

Television, single episode in a series.

Restak, R. M. (1989). Depression and mood (D. Sage, Director). In J. Sameth (Producer), *The mind.* New York: WNET.

Doctoral Dissertations and Theses

Doctoral dissertation, unpublished.

Seltzer, M. (1990). *The use of data augmentation in fitting hierarchical models to educational data.* Unpublished doctoral dissertation, University of Chicago.

Doctoral dissertation, abstracted in *Dissertation Abstracts International,* available from a university.

Nitsch, K. E. (1977). *Structuring decontextualized forms of knowledge.* (Doctoral dissertation, Vanderbilt University, 1977). *Dissertation Abstracts International, 38B,* 3935.

Thesis, master's, unpublished.

Klausmeier, H. J. (1947). *An experiment with two methods of teaching social studies in high school.* Unpublished master's thesis, Indiana State University.

Thesis, honors, unpublished.

Rigney, J.C. (1962). *A developmental study of cognitive equivalence transformations and their use in the acquisition and processing of information.* Unpublished honors thesis, Radcliffe College.

Electronic Media

In 1994 when the *Publication Manual of APA* was published, a style had not been firmly established for citing electronic sources of material. Since then a vast amount of electronic material has become available and much more is appearing. Responding to this burgeoning field, the American Psychological Association in 1999 produced electronically *Electronic Reference Formats Recommended by the American Psychological Association.* This document will very likely continue to give the APA approved style for citing electronic material in the reference list and in the text for the next years.

The complete document is reproduced in Appendix D of this *Handbook.* It has five main parts: Citing Email, Communications; Citing a Web Site; Citing Specific Documents on a Web Site; Citing Articles and Abstracts from Electronic Databases–CD-ROM, On-line, Accessed via the Web; and Web Citations in the Text. Examples follow for Citing Specific Documents on a Web Site:

An article from the *APA Monitor* (a newspaper):

Sleek, S. (1996, January). Psychologists build a culture of peace. *APA Monitor*, pp. 1, 33. Retrieved January 25, 1996 from the World Wide Web: http://www/apa.org/monitor/peacea.html

An abstract:

Rosenthal, R. (1995). *State of New Jersey v. Margaret Kelly Michaels:* An overview [Abstract]. *Psychology, Public Policy and Law, 1,* 247-271. Retrieved January 25, 1996 from the World Wide Web: http://www.apa.org/journals/ab1.html

This document:

> *Electronic reference formats recommended by the American Psychological Association.* (1999, November 19). Washington, DC: American Psychological Association. Retrieved November 19, 1999 from the World Wide Web: http//www.apa.org/journals/webref.html

In the 1994 *Publication Manual of APA,* the guides for citing electronic material were based on Li and Crane's (1993) *Electronic Style: A Guide for Citing Electronic Information.* Li and Crane (1996) brought out a revised edition of the book titled *Electronic Styles: A Handbook for Citing Electronic Information.* The 1996 book has more complete instructions and many more examples than the 1999 APA document previously cited. However, the format in Li and Crane (1996) differs from that of the 1999 APA document as may be seen by comparing the prior APA examples with the following example from Li and Crane:

> Inada, K. (1995). A Buddhist response to the nature of human rights. *Journal of Buddhist Ethics* [Online], 2, 9 paragraphs. Available: http://www.cac.psu.edu/jbe/twocont.html [1995, June 21]. (p. 31).

The availability of computer software, similar to on-line information, is increasing very rapidly. However, the style for citing software will probably not change much from the following:

> Miller, M. E. (1993). The Interactive Tester (Version 4.0). [Computer software]. Westminster, CA: Psytech Services.

Statutes, Legislative Materials, Court Decisions, and Executive Orders

The amount of published legal material is vast and it is accumulating rapidly. The basic source on referencing legal material is *The Bluebook: A Uniform System of Citation* (1996).

Most writers of research reports do not cite legal material. However, examples of references and also in-text citations for the four main classes of material follow. More examples are given in the *APA Publication Manual* (1994). A writer who is reviewing the legal literature on a topic might well consult a legal expert for assistance in preparing the references. (The material in parentheses after some of the examples that follow clarifies abbreviations in the examples; it is not part of the examples.)

Statutes.

Americans With Disabilities Act of 1990, Pub. L. No. 101-335, 104 Stat. 328 (1991). (104 *Stat.* 328 = *United States Statutes at Large,* Volume 104, page 328.)

In-text citation
Americans with Disabilities Act (1990)
(Americans with Disabilities Act of 1990)

Legislative material, full hearing.

Famine in Africa: Hearing before the Committee on Foreign Relations, Senate, 99th Cong., 1st Sess. (1985).

In-text citation
Famine in Africa (1985)
(*Famine in Africa,* 1985)

Supreme Court decision recorded in United States Reports.

Associated Press v. United States, 326 U. S. 1 (1944).
(326 U. S. 1 = Volume 326 of the *United States Reports* starting on page 1.)

In-text citation
Associated Press v. United States (1944)
(*Associated Press v. United States,* 1944)

Supreme Court decision recorded in *Supreme Court Reporter.*

Maryland v. Craig, 110 S. Ct. 3157 (1990).
(110 S. Ct. 3157 = Volume 110 of the *Supreme Court Reporter* starting on page 3157.)

In-text citation
Maryland v. Craig (1990)
(*Maryland v. Craig,* 1990)

Case appealed to a court of appeals.

United States v. Rouse, F.3d 360 (8th Cir. 1996).
    (F.3d 360 = *Federal Court Reporter*, Third Series starting on page 360.)

In-text citation
    United States v. Rouse (1996)
    (*United States v. Rouse,* 1996)

Case appealed to a state supreme court.

State v. Michaels, 136 N. J. 299, 642 A.2d 1372 (1994).
    (136 N.J. 299 = Volume 136 of the *New Jersey Reports* starting on page 299.)

In-text citation
    State v. Michaels (1994)
    (*State v. Michaels,* 1994)

Executive order.

Exec. Order No. 12804, 3 C.F.R. 298 (1992).
    (3 CFR 298 = Volume 3 of the *Code of Federal Regulations,* page 298.)

In-text citation
    Executive Order No. 12804 (1992)
    (Executive Order No. 12804, 1992)

Sample Reference List

In the reference list, the entries are listed alphabetically. A one-author work precedes a multiauthor work that begins with the same surname as the one-author work. Works by the same author(s) are entered by the year of publication, the earliest year first. References by the same author(s) with the same year of publication are ordered by the title of the work, excluding A or The; lowercase letters–*a, b,* and so on–are placed immediately after the year within the parentheses. Works with group authors or with no author are entered by the first significant word in the name, except that the full names of official groups are given.

Exhibit 7.2 shows implementation of the preceding guides. The list includes different categories of authorship and the main kinds of works typically appearing in reference lists of research articles.

The references listed in Exhibit 7.2 are identical to those listed later in Exhibit A1, except that those in Exhibit A1 conform to the editorial style of the 1993 *Chicago Manual of Style.*

Exhibit 7.2. Sample Reference List That Conforms to the Editorial Style of the 1994 *Publication Manual of the American Psychological Association*

American Association of University Women. (1992). *How schools short change girls: The AAUW report.* Washington, DC: Author.

Clarke-Stewart, K. A., Gruber, C. P., & Fitzgerald, L. M. (1994). *Children at home and in day care.* Hillsdale, NJ: Erlbaum.

Downright, A. B. (1993). Narrative diffusion and the professional editor. (Doctoral dissertation, University of Chicago, 1993). *Dissertation Abstracts International, 52,* 3245A-3246A.

Fredrick, W. C., & Klausmeier, H. J. (1968a). Concept identification as a function of the number of relevant and irrelevant dimensions, presentation method, and salience. *Psychological Reports, 23,* 631-634.

Fredrick, W. C., & Klausmeier, H. J. (1968b). Instructions and labels in a concept attainment task. *Psychological Reports, 23,* 1339–1342.

Goode, E. (1998, November 3). New hope for losers in the battle to stay awake. *The New York Times,* pp. D1, 8.

Klausmeier, H. J. (1968). Essential or helpful [Review of the book *Essentials of learning: An overview for students of education.* 2nd ed.]. *Contemporary Psychology, 13,* 574.

Klausmeier, H. J. (1977, August). *Individual differences in cognitive development during the school years.* Paper presented at the meeting of the American Psychological Association, San Francisco.

Klausmeier, H. J. (1979). Experience and cognitive development. *Proceedings of the International Symposium on Physics, Biology, and Mathematics: Different Approaches in an Integrated Curriculum for the Primary School* (pp. 33-71). Rome: Italian Academy of Science.

Klausmeier, H. J. (1985). *Educational psychology* (5th ed.). New York: Harper & Row.

Klausmeier, H. J. (1991). *Concept learning and concept teaching.* (Cassette Recording No. 91-033). Washington, DC: American Psychological Association.

Klausmeier, H. J. (1992). Concept learning and concept teaching. *Educational Psychologist, 27,* 267-286.

Klausmeier, H. J. (1996). The role of the researcher in educational improvement: A retrospective analysis. In C. B. Benbow & D. Lubinski (Eds.), *Intellectual talent: Psychometric and social issues* (pp. 99-115). Baltimore, MD: The Johns Hopkins University Press.

Klausmeier, H. J., & Allen, P.S. (1978). *Cognitive development of children and youth: A longitudinal study.* New York: Academic Press.

Klausmeier, H. J., & Harris, C. W. (Eds.). (1966). *Analyses of concept learning.* New York: Academic Press.

Merkin, D. (1998, November 9). Freud rising. *New Yorker,* 50-55.

Morris, J. A. (Ed.). (1997). *Practicing psychology in rural areas: Hospital privileges and collaborative care.* Washington, DC: American Psychological Association.

Piaget, J. (1971). *Psychology and epistemology: Towards a theory of knowledge.* (A. Rosin, Trans.). New York: Viking Press.

Sandoval, J., Frisby, C., Geisinger, K., Ramos-Grenier, J., & Scheuneman, J. (Eds.). (1998). *Test interpretation and diversity: Achieving equity in assessment.* Washington, DC: American Psychological Association.

Seltzer, M. (1990). *The use of data augmentation in fitting hierarchical models to educational data.* Unpublished doctoral dissertation, University of Chicago.

Woodall, W. G., Davis, D. K., & Sahin, H. (1983). From the boob tube to the black box: Television news comprehension from an information processing perspective. *Journal of Broadcasting, 27,* 1-23.

Chapter 8

SUBMITTING A MANUSCRIPT AND
RESPONDING TO EDITORIAL REVIEW

Preparing a manuscript for submission to a journal editor, submitting it, responding to an editor's evaluation of the manuscript, reviewing and returning the copyedited manuscript, and reading and returning the typeset proof are author responsibilities. The author also has obligations after an article has been published.

Preparing and Submitting a Manuscript

The guidelines that follow, unless otherwise noted, are in accord with the *Publication Manual of the American Psychological Association* (American Psychological Association, 1994). Most journals in psychology, education, and related fields follow the *Publication Manual of APA*; however, some do not. Accordingly, manuscript authors should examine the most recent issue of the journal to which they submit a manuscript to identify the specific requirements of the journal. Examples of requirements were given in Chapter 2.

Word Processing a Manuscript

Care in preparing a manuscript increases the prospects for its acceptance. Journal editors and manuscript reviewers expect to receive attractive manuscripts that meet a journal's style requirements. The requirements that follow are widely accepted, regardless of the editorial style demanded:

- Use 8-1/2 x 11 in. high-quality white paper.
- Make the size of the type 12 points. Do not used a compressed typeface or settings that would decrease the spacing between letters or words.
- Use the special characters on the keyboard, such as the Greek letters and mathematical signs and symbols. Use the numbers 0 and 1, not the let-

ters O and 1 (el). Underline everything that is to appear in italics in the published article.

- Double space the entire manuscript. Put no more than 27 lines on a page. Do not use single-spacing or one-and-one-half spacing for a table or any other part of a manuscript.
- The margins must be one inch for the top, bottom, and the left and right sides of the page. Do not justify the right margin.
- Indent the first line of every paragraph of the text and the footnotes five to seven spaces. Not to be indented are the first line of the abstract, block quotations, titles and headings, table titles and notes, and figure captions.

A journal publisher may require authors to submit the electronic word processing file with the paper copies of the manuscript and also an unformatted ASCII file. The ASCII file may be used throughout the review and publication process. Consult the most recent issue of the journal to learn the requirements and how to proceed. If more information is desired, consult the journal editor.

Title page. Three items are entered on the title page: the running head (i.e., an abbreviated title of the manuscript), the title, and the byline (i.e., author's name and institutional affiliation). Also, the manuscript page header (i.e., the first two or three words of the title), and 1 for the page number are placed in the upper right-hand corner of the title page.

Put the running head, all letters in uppercase, at the top of the page. Place it flush left, below the manuscript page header.

Enter the title in uppercase and lowercase letters (e.g., Children's Fantasies), centered on the page. If the title is two or more lines, double-space between the lines.

Enter the name of the author in uppercase and lowercase letters, centered, one double-space below the title. Place the author's institutional affiliation, centered, on the next double-spaced line below the author's name. If there are two or more authors, refer to an issue of the journal to identify the style for entering the names and organizations. (If the manuscript is to get masked review, the journal editor will remove the title page before submitting the manuscript to reviewers.)

Abstract. Double-space the abstract. Begin it on a separate page. Prepare it as a single paragraph without a paragraph indent. Place the manuscript page header and the page number 2 in the upper right-hand corner of the page.

An abstract should be readable and self-contained, giving a concise summary of a study. Including key words in the abstract will help others locate the abstract in a database of abstracts.

An abstract of an empirical study should not exceed 960 characters and spaces, approximately 120 words. It should present the problem; the participants, including pertinent characteristics; the method, including data-gathering procedures, tests, and similar information; the findings with statistical significance levels; and conclusions. A citation in the abstract must include the author's surname and initials and the year of publication.

An abstract of a review article should not exceed 100 words. Include in the abstract the topic, the purpose and scope, the sources of information, and the conclusions.

Preparing an abstract requires attention to details. To save space, abbreviate freely but be aware that abbreviations requiring explanation in the text must also be explained in the abstract. Do not spell out any number except one that might begin a sentence. Try to rewrite a sentence so that a number is not the first word. Use verbs rather than nouns and the active voice rather than the passive. However, do not use *I* or *we*.

Page numbering and manuscript page headers. Number the pages of the text and accompanying material (i.e., references, author note, etc.) consecutively, except the figures, starting with the title page. Put the page numbers in Arabic numerals in the upper right-hand corner of the page. If a page must be removed or added, renumber the pages; do not give a page two numbers (e.g., 7,8) or add a letter after a page number (e.g., 9a). Identify each page, except for figures, with the manuscript page header. Place the header above the page number or five spaces to the left of it.

Order of text and other pages. Arrange the pages numbered consecutively in the following order:

- title, author(s), institutional affiliation(s), and running head for publication—on a separate page, numbered 1
- abstract—on a separate page, numbered 2
- text—start on a separate page, numbered 3
- references—start on a separate page
- appendixes—start on a separate page
- author note—start on a separate page
- footnotes—listed together, start on a separate page
- tables—start each one on a separate page
- figure captions—listed together, start on a separate page
- figures—put each one on a separate page (these pages are not numbered).

Copies. Journals require the original copy of a manuscript and two or more additional copies. The glossy or laser prints of any figures must be included. One set of photocopies of the figures is required. See the last issue of the selected journal for instructions.

Cover Letter to Journal Editor

A short cover letter should give general information about the study (e.g., whether it has been presented at a meeting or whether a related manuscript has been submitted for publication). APA style also calls for specific information, including the title, the number of pages, and the number of figures and tables. At the time a manuscript is accepted, the requirements include written certification of authorship and verification that the treatment of the participants meets ethical standards. Permissions to reproduce material should be enclosed. The author's phone number, fax number, E-mail address, and address for correspondence should be supplied. See Appendix C for an example of a cover letter.

Responding to Editorial Review

The review process varies among journal publishers. Only the editor, an associate editor, or the publisher may review a manuscript. However, in many journals in psychology, education, and related fields, the journal editor and two or more scholars review the manuscript. The reviewers provide the editor their evaluation of the quality of the manuscript and its appropriateness for the journal. The editor then decides whether to accept the manuscript, accept it conditional on satisfactory revision, reject it encouraging revision, or reject it. Appendix C has examples of editorial reviews and also the forms that manuscript reviewers use to report their evaluations.

Revising a Manuscript Accepted Conditional on Revision

The weaknesses in a manuscript leading to its being accepted conditional on revision vary for empirical, review, and theoretical studies. The following discussion deals mainly with empirical studies and is presented according to main parts of a manuscript. Weaknesses related to the substance of a study precede those pertaining to the writing style.

Introductions often have either of two weaknesses. One is that not all of the hypotheses are related to the problem. Another is that the review of the literature is incomplete or it includes some studies that are irrelevant.

Reviewers often find weaknesses in the methods employed in a study. They base their evaluations on questions such as these: Are the data-gathering instruments reliable and valid? Are they sufficient for answering the research question or for testing the hypotheses? Is the data analysis appropriate for the research problem and the data collected? Is the design of the study appropriate? A flaw in any of these areas invariably leads to acceptance conditional on revision or to rejection.

The last part of a manuscript usually presents the results of the study, conclusions, and recommendations. Manuscripts accepted conditional on revision usually have flaws such as the following: Results are stated that do not follow from the analysis of the data or not all of the results are reported. Incorrect conclusions are drawn. The limitations of the study are not given. Unwarranted recommendations are presented.

Manuscript authors can readily deal with the preceding weaknesses in the introductory and final sections of a manuscript. The flaws for the methods section may prove more difficult to remedy. Regardless of the ease or difficulty, it is advisable to revise a manuscript. The likelihood for getting a revised manuscript accepted is much greater than it is for an original manuscript.

A manuscript having none of the preceding problems may be accepted conditional on revision because of the inadequacy of the writing style. For example, in the introduction the problem is not stated clearly or the review of the literature is not appropriately concise, fully integrated, or connected directly to the problem. In the methods section, the procedures are not presented clearly, confusing the reader. Similar inadequacies are found in the presentation of the results, conclusions, and recommendations. Also, there are errors in grammar and biased language is used. Chapter 3 of this *Handbook* has guides for eliminating these problems;

Options for Publication of a Rejected Manuscript

Journal editors reject manuscripts for different reasons. The most frequently given reasons and one or more options for responding follow.

One basis for rejection is that a study does not contribute to an area of interest of the journal. The best option here is to identify a journal that publishes the kind of subject matter of the study and submit the manuscript to it. Journal editors returning a rejected manuscript often suggest suitable journals.

An editor evaluates a study as not making a significant contribution to the field. One option is for the author to send the manuscript to a different journal. Another possibility is to make the significance of the study more apparent and submit the revised manuscript to a different journal.

An editor rejects a manuscript because of weakness in the review, the method, or the results. Getting this study published calls for eliminating the weakness and transmitting the manuscript to the same or a different journal.

Besides having weaknesses in the content of the study, manuscript rejection also follows from serious deficiencies in writing style, grammar, editorial style, or manuscript preparation. In general, rejections for these causes are usually accompanied with encouragement for revision. Options here are to make the revisions and transmit the revised manuscript either to the same journal or to a different one.

In addition to the preceding, two other options may be appropriate. In some instances, the author may reduce the scope of the study and prepare an abbreviated report. In other instances, the journal to which the manuscript was initially sent may have an appeal process. An appeal may be undertaken.

Chapter 2, dealing with preparing to write a manuscript, highlights the importance of selecting a journal that publishes the kind of subject matter of the author's study and that has a suitable acceptance rate. This becomes even more important when selecting a journal to which to submit a manuscript that was initially rejected.

Manuscript authors should recognize that there are differences among journals in encouraging revision and resubmission of manuscripts and also in the feedback provided to the author. The two manuscript evaluation forms in Appendix C show these differences.

Doing nothing after receiving a rejection notice is to be avoided. Rather, a rejection should be viewed as a challenge to pursue vigorously. This is how major league baseball players regard a similar situation. After striking out, they seek help from the batting coach or a star hitter. They continue to take their turns at bat and persist until they get a hit.

Securing Expert Assistance

Whether a manuscript is accepted conditional on satisfactory revision or rejected, the manuscript author might well get an experienced author who has served as a manuscript reviewer to critique the editor's evaluation and the manuscript. The expert can analyze the manuscript and provide suggestions regarding an option to pursue and revisions to be made, if necessary.

Manuscript Review and Proofreading

Manuscript review, reading proof, and production of an article vary among publishers. In a typical pattern, after a manuscript is accepted for publication, it is copyedited and returned to the author for review. After reviewing and making changes, the author returns the corrected manuscript for typesetting. The typeset proof is returned to the author for final reading.

Reviewing the Copyedited Manuscript

For many journals there is both a journal editor and a copy editor. Both editors may make minor changes in the manuscript dealing with style, form, and similar matters but not the substance. The marked up, copyedited manuscript is returned to the author along with instructions for making changes in it.

The copyedited manuscript requires careful review to make sure that the editors have not changed any substantive aspects of the study. The levels of headings and the markup of tables and statistics should be checked to make sure they are correct. Be aware that any change made after submitting the reviewed manuscript is at the author's expense.

Reading the Typeset Proof

The author submits the reviewed copyedited manuscript for typesetting. After the typesetting is completed, the copyedited manuscript and two copies of the typeset proof are sent to the author.

There should be no corrections or changes of any kind required in the typeset proof. However, read the original copy of the proof carefully. Check to see that it agrees with the copyedited manuscript. Make only changes in the proof that are essential. Return the original copy of the proof and the copyedited manuscript. Keep a copy of the proof.

Editors, journal production staff, and authors use proofreaders' marks to indicate corrections on the page proof. They use the marks in pair, placing one where the change is to be made and the other in the margin closest to the change. The *Merriam-Webster's Collegiate Dictionary* (1998, p. 934) lists the marks and gives examples of their use.

After Publication of the Article

Keep the original data and the description of the participants, procedure, analysis of data, and similar information for a minimum of five years after the article is published. If important information in the published article is incorrect or has been omitted, prepare a correction notice and submit it to the journal editor. It is advisable to confer with the journal editor in advance to ascertain whether the correction notice will be published and what is required for preparing and submitting it.

Author Responsibilities

The author is responsible for everything concerned with the manuscript. This includes the substance and all matters pertaining to writing style and editorial style. Preparing the manuscript, reviewing the copyedited manuscript, and reading the page proof are author obligations.

If there are two or more authors who participate in the reviewing and proofreading, the first author is responsible for incorporating the other authors' suggestions in the copy of the material that is transmitted to the journal editor or other members of the publisher's staff. Likewise, the first author is responsible for keeping the data and related material for five years, responding to correspondence, and ordering and paying for reprints.

Proofreading is usually a pleasant experience. Not much work is required, and the author knows that an article will soon appear. On the other hand, responding to editorial review is often stressful, particularly when a negative evaluation from the journal editor seems unwarranted. It may be helpful to know that journal editors and manuscript reviewers would rather accept manuscripts than reject them. These scholars take their work seriously. They do the best they can to deal fairly with the manuscript authors and, at the same time, meet the demands of the journal publisher.

REFERENCES

American Educational Research Association. (1999). AERA extended course participation stipends. *Educational Researcher, 28*(8), 42.

American national standard for metric practice. (1992). New York: American National Standards Institute.

American Psychological Association. (1977, June). *Guidelines for nonsexist language in APA journals.* [Reprint of section 2.12 of the 3rd ed. of the Publication Manual of the American Psychological Association]. Washington, DC: Author.

American Psychological Association, Board of Ethnic and Minority Affairs and Publications and Communications Board. (1989). *Guidelines for avoiding racial/ethnic bias in language* (Draft). Unpublished manuscript. Washington, DC: Author.

American Psychological Association, Committee on Lesbian and Gay Concerns. (1991). *Avoiding heterosexual bias in language.* Unpublished manuscript. Washington, DC: Author.

American Psychological Association. (1992a). Ethical principles of psychologists and code of conduct. *American Psychologist, 47,* 1597-1611.

American Psychological Association, Committee on Disability Issues in Psychology. (1992b). *Guidelines for nonhandicapping language in APA journals.* Unpublished manuscript. Washington, DC: Author.

American Psychological Association. (1994). *Publication manual of the American Psychological Association* (4th ed.). Washington, DC: Author.

American Psychological Association. (1997). *Journals in psychology: A resource listing for authors* (5th ed.). Washington, DC: Author.

The bluebook: A uniform system of citation (16th ed.). (1996). Cambridge, MA: Harvard Law Review Association.

Canter, M. B., Bennett, B. E., Jones, S. E., & Nagy, T. F. (1994). *Ethics for psychologists: A commentary on the APA ethics code.* Washington, DC: American Psychological Association.

Chapman, R. L. (1996). *Roget's international thesaurus* (5th ed.). New York: HarperCollins.

Electronic reference formats recommended by the American Psychological Association.
(1999, November 19). Washington, DC: Retrieved June 22, 2000, from the
World Wide Web: http://www.apa.org/journals/webref.html

Fine, M. A., & Kurdek, L. A. (1993). Reflections on determining authorship
credit and authorship order on faculty-student collaborations. *American
Psychologist, 48,* 1141-1147.

Furnish, B. (1996). *Write right.* Bloomington, IN: Phi Delta Kappa.

Henson, K. T. (1999). Writing for professional journals. *Phi Delta Kappan, 80,*
780-783.

Kane, T. S. (1994). *The new Oxford guide to writing.* New York: Oxford
University Press.

Li, X., & Crane, N. B. (1993). *Electronic style: A guide to citing electronic information.* Westport, CT: Meckler.

Li, X., & Crane, N. B. (1996). *Electronic styles: A handbook for citing electronic
information.* Medford, NJ: Information Today, Inc.

Maggio, R. (1991). *The dictionary of bias-free usage: A guide to nondiscriminatory
language.* Phoenix, AZ: Oryx Press.

Meltzoff, J. (1998). *Critical thinking about research: Psychology and related fields.*
Washington, DC: American Psychological Association.

Merriam-Webster's collegiate dictionary (10th ed.). (1998). Springfield, MA:
Merriam-Webster.

Nagy, T. F. (1999). *Ethics in plain English: An illustrative casebook for psychologists.* Washington, DC: American Psychological Association.

Nicol, A., & Pexman, P. A. (1999). *Presenting your findings: A practical guide for
creating tables.* Washington, DC: American Psychological Association.

Schaie, K. W. (1993). Ageist language in psychological research. *American
Psychologist, 48,* 49-51.

Strunk, W., Jr. (1999). *The elements of style.* New York: Bartleby.com. Retrieved
July 1, 2000 from the World Wide Web: http://www.bartleby.com/141/

Strunk, W., Jr., & White, E. B. (1999). *The elements of style.* Needham Heights,
MA: Allyn and Bacon.

University of Chicago Press. (1993). *The Chicago manual of style: The essential
guide for writers, editors, and publishers* (14th ed.). Chicago: Author.

Warren, T. L. (1992). *Words into type* (4th ed.). Englewood Cliffs, NJ: Prentice
Hall.

*Webster's third new international dictionary, unabridged: The great library of the
English language.* (1993). Springfield, MA: Merriam-Webster.

Wiersma, W. (2000). *Research methods in education: An introduction.* Needham
Heights, MA: Allyn and Bacon.

READINGS

Allison, A., & Frongia, T. (1992). *The grad student's guide to getting published.* Englewood Cliffs, NJ: Prentice Hall.

Alton-Lee, A. (1998). A troubleshooter's checklist for prospective authors derived from reviewers' critical feedback. *Teaching and Teacher Education: An International Journal of Research and Studies, 14*(8), 887-890.

American Educational Research Association. (ND). Washington, DC: Author. Retrieved from the World Wide Web: www.aera.net (This web site contains tables of contents and abstracts of articles for all current and prior issues of journals of the American Educational Research Association.)

American Mathematical Society. (1990). *Manual for authors of mathematical papers* (8th ed.). Providence, RI: Author.

American Psychological Association. (1984). *Preparing abstracts for journal articles and Psychological Abstracts* (Draft). Washington, DC: Author.

Bates, J. D. (1997). *Writing with precision: America's classic guide to English* (7th ed.). Washington, DC: Acropolis Books.

Bersoff, D. N. (1999). *Ethical conflicts in psychology* (2nd ed.). Washington, DC: American Psychological Association.

Eichorn, D. H., & VanderBos, G. R. (1985). Dissemination of scientific and professional knowledge: Journal publication within the APA. *American Psychologist, 40,* 1309-1316.

Frankel, M. S. (1993). Professional societies and responsible research conduct. In *Responsible science: Ensuring the integrity of the research process* (Vol. 2, pp. 26-49). Washington, DC: National Academy Press.

Gibaldi, J. (1998). *MLA style manual and guide to scholarly publishing* (2nd ed.). New York: Modern Language Association of America.

Gorrell, D. (1994). *A writer's handbook, from A to Z* (2nd ed.). Needham Heights, MA: Allyn and Bacon.

Knatterud, M. E. (1991, February). Writing with the patient in mind: Don't add insult to injury. *American Medical Writers Association Journal, 6,* 10-17.

Lowman, R. L. (1998). *The ethical practice of psychology in organizations* (2nd ed.). Washington, DC: American Psychological Association.

Schwartz, M. (1995). *Guidelines for bias-free writing.* Bloomington, IN: Indiana University Press.

Zinsser, W. (1996). *On writing well: An informal guide to writing nonfiction* (4th ed.). New York: HarperCollins.

APPENDIX A. REFERENCE CITATIONS IN THE TEXT AND REFERENCES IN THE REFERENCE LIST THAT CONFORM TO THE 1993 *CHICAGO MANUAL OF STYLE*

CONTENTS

Reference Citations in the Text 111
  Basic Form of Citations 111
    One author 111
    Two or three authors 111
    Two different authors with the same last name and the same
      date 111
    A work by two family members with the same name 111
    Author(s) rather than the work 111
    More than three authors 112
    More than three authors when there is another work of the
      same date 112
    Groups as author 112
    Government agency as author 112
    Page(s), figure, appendix, and note 112
    Volume and page number(s), one volume, more than one
      volume 113
    Two or more sources in one parenthetical citation 113
    Additional works by the same author without and with pages
      given 113
  Three Ways to Enter Text Citations 113
    Citation, enclosed in parentheses 113
    Citation of other authors(s), date enclosed in parentheses 113
    Citation of self as author, date not enclosed in parentheses 113

References in the Reference List 114
  Books 114
    One author 114
    Two authors 114
    Three authors 114
    Groups as author 114
    In process of publication 115
    Non-English 115
    More than three authors 115
    Anonymous work 115
    One editor 115
    Two editors 115
    More than three editors 115
    Translated 115
  Parts of a Book 116
    Book part, author of part also author of book 116
    Book chapter, author of chapter also author of book 116
    Book chapter, one author, two editors 116
    Foreword to a book 116
  Editions, Multivolumes, Editors, and Series 117
  Periodicals 117
    Journal article, no author 117
    Journal article, one author 117
    Journal article, two authors 118
    Journal article, three authors 118
    Journal article, more than three authors 118
    Journal, issue number, month or season 118
    Magazine article 118
    Daily newspaper article, discontinuous pages 118
  Reviews in Periodicals 118
    Review, book 118
    Review, movie 119
  Personal Communications 119
  Unpublished Material 119
    Dissertations and theses 119
    Papers and symposium contributions 119
  Special Types of References 120

Public Documents 120
  Hearings 120
  Laws, Public Acts, and Statutes 120
    Slip laws 121
    Statutes cited in the U. S. Statutes at Large 121
    Statutes entered in the U. S. Code 121
  Executive Department Documents 121
    Federal Court Decisions 122
    International Bodies 122

Nonbook Materials 123

Computer Software and Electronic Documents .124
  Computer Software 124
  Electronic Documents 125

Sample Reference List 126

APPENDIX A. REFERENCE CITATIONS IN THE TEXT AND REFERENCES IN THE REFERENCE LIST THAT CONFORM TO THE 1993 *CHICAGO MANUAL OF STYLE*

Reference Citations in the Text

Basic Form of Citations

The basic form is to give the author's last name and the year of publication in the text and at the end of block quotations. An exception is to give the authors' initials for two or more works by different authors with the same last name and the same date. Relative to the basic form, the term author refers to an author, editor, compiler, or organization.

One author.

(Klausmeier 1996)

Two or three authors.

(Klausmeier and Allen 1978)

(Klausmeier, Rossmiller, and Saily 1977)

Two different authors with the same last name and the same date.

(J. Smith and L. Smith 1999)

A work by two family members with the same last name.

(Harris and Harris 1971)

Author(s) rather than the work.

The Harrises (1971) agree that concept learning . . .

More than three authors.

(Eccles et al. 1993)

More than three authors when there is another work of the same date.

(Eccles, Wigfield, Midgley, Reuman, MacIver, and Feldhaufer (1993) or (Eccles, Wigfield et al. 1993)

Groups as author. Longer names of groups may be shortened. The shortened version must agree with the opening part of the entry in the reference list. The references for the examples that follow are listed later under Groups as Author.

(AAUW 1992)
(Carnegie Task Force 1986)
(Edmonton Public Schools 1981)
(NAEP 1990)
(Psychological Corporation 1992)

Government agency as author. The names of government agencies vary in length; some are very long. Accordingly, authors and editors devise the text citations. Shorter names are cited in full; longer names are shortened. The date is given as it is for other authors. The form devised must be consistent throughout a manuscript.

Page(s), figure, appendix, and note. Only one parenthetical citation is needed when more than one reference to a source is made in a paragraph. In a paragraph, the first citation of different pages of the same source gives the author and date; later citations give only the page. The following examples are for the first or only citation in a paragraph.

(Klausmeier and Allen 1978, 160)

(Klausmeier, Rossmiller, and Saily 1977, 56-76)

(Klausmeier 1995, fig. 2.1)
(Klausmeier, Rossmiller, and Saily 1978, app. A)

(Klausmeier and Loughlin 1961, 149n)

Volume and page number(s), one volume, more than one volume.
The volume number is not italicized and is followed with a colon. A volume cited without a page number requires the abbreviation vol. to be entered.

(Klausmeier and Loughlin 1961, 52:148-152)

(Smith 1999, 1:52-70, 2:110-148)

(Klausmeier and Loughlin 1961, vol. 52)

Two or more sources in one parenthetical citation.

(Klausmeier and Allen 1978; Klausmeier, Lipham, and Daresh 1983)

Additional works by the same author without and with pages given.

(Klausmeier 1972, 1975)

(Klausmeier 1972, 110; 1975, 100-112)

Three Ways to Enter Text Citations

The preceding citations are enclosed in parentheses. However, whether to enclose sources in parentheses depends on how the author refers to the source and whether the source is a publication of the author.

Citation, enclosed in parentheses.

Two longitudinal studies of children's development (Hooper and Swinton 1978; Klausmeier and Allen 1978) draw different conclusions about . . .

Citation of other authors, date enclosed in parentheses.

Hooper and Swinton (1978) identify . . .

Citation of self as author, date not enclosed in parentheses.

In our study of children's development, Klausmeier and Allen 1978 conclude . . .

References in the Reference List

Books

The basic form for books in the reference list is as follows: (a) the author's name, (b) the date, (c) the title with the first word of the main title, the first word of the subtitle, proper nouns and proper adjectives, and I capitalized, (d) the place of publication, and (e) the publisher. The initials of the first author follow the surname; those of the second and later authors precede the surname. The date is not enclosed in parentheses.

One author.

Klausmeier, H. J. 1985. *Educational psychology.* 5th ed. New York: Harper & Row.

Two authors.

Klausmeier, H. J., and P. S. Allen. 1978. *Cognitive development of children and youth: A longitudinal study.* New York: Academic Press.

Three authors.

Clarke-Stewart, K. A., C. P. Gruber, and L. M. Fitzgerald. 1994. *Children at home and in day care.* Hillsdale, NJ: Erlbaum.

Groups as author.

American Association of University Women. 1992. *How schools short change girls: The AAUW report.* New York: Marlowe.

Carnegie Task Force on Teaching as a Profession. 1986. *A nation prepared: Teachers for the 21st century.* New York: Carnegie Forum on Education and the Economy.

Edmonton Public Schools Board. 1981. *Edmonton Public Schools spelling achievement tests.* Edmonton, Alberta, Canada: Edmonton Public Schools Board.

National Assessment of Educational Progress. 1990. *The fifth national mathematics assessment.* Denver, CO: National Assessment of Educational Progress.

Psychological Corporation. 1992. *Wechsler Individual Achievement Test manual.* San Antonio, TX: Psychological Corporation.

In process of publication. Forthcoming or In press is entered in place of an actual publication date.

Non-English book.

Skaalvik, S. 1995. *Voksne med lese–og skrivevansker forteller om sine skoleer-faringer* (School experiences among adults with reading and writing problems). Trondheim, Norway: Norsk voksenpedagogisk institutt.

More than three authors.

Coleman, J., E. Campbell, C. Hobson, J. McPartland, A. Mood, J. Weinfield, and R. York. 1966. *Equality of educational opportunity.* Washington, DC: U. S. Government Printing Office.

Anonymous work. Begin with the title of the work if the author's name cannot be identified. Do not use Anonymous.

One editor.

Morris, J. A., ed. 1997. *Practicing psychology in rural areas: Hospital privileges and collaborative care.* Washington, DC: American Psychological Association.

Two editors.

Pressman, M. R., and W. C. Orr, eds. 1998. *Understanding sleep: the evaluation and treatment of sleep disorders.* Washington, DC: American Psychological Association.

More than three editors.

Sandoval, J., C. Frisby, K. Geisinger, J. Ramos-Grenier, and J. Scheuneman, eds. 1998. *Test interpretation and diversity: Achieving equity in assessment.* Washington, DC: American Psychological Association.

Translated.

Piaget, J. 1971. *Psychology and epistemology: Towards a theory of knowledge.* Translated by A. S. Rosin. New York: Viking Press.

Parts of a Book

When a chapter or other part of a book is cited, the title of the part ends with a period and is followed by In and the title of the book. If the part (e.g., Chap. 5 in) is identified by part and number, it replaces In preceding the title of the book.

Book part, authors of part also authors of book.

Klausmeier, H. J., J. M. Lipham, and J. C. Daresh. 1983. Instructional programming for the individual student. In *The renewal and improvement of secondary education.* Lanham, MD: University Press of America.

Book chapter, author of chapter also author of book.

Klausmeier, H. J. 1985. Personality integration and classroom discipline. Chap. 13 in *Educational psychology*, 5th ed. New York: Harper & Row.

Book chapter, one author, two editors.

Klausmeier, H. J. 1996. The role of the researcher in educational improvement: A retrospective analysis. Chap. 5 in *Intellectual talent: Psychometric and social issues*, edited by C. B. Benbow and D. Lubinski. Baltimore, MD: The Johns Hopkins University Press.

The text citations that follow for the preceding parts of a book include the pages; the chapter is not necessary:

(Klausmeier, Lipham, and Daresh 1983, 1-31)
(Klausmeier 1985, 407-436)
(Klausmeier 1996, 99-115)

Foreword to a book.

Harrington, F. H. 1990. Foreword to *The Wisconsin Center for Education Research: Twenty-five years of knowledge generation and educational improvement*, by H. J. Klausmeier and Associates. Madison, WI: Wisconsin Center for Education Research.

Editions, Multivolumes, Editors, and Series

The number of the edition follows the title, for example, *Educational psychology*, 5th ed. New York: Harper & Row.

The volume number follows the title, for example, *Survey of American humor*, Vol. 2, *Humor of the American Midwest*. Boston: Plenum Press.

The indicator for editorship of a book follows the name(s), for example, Klausmeier, H. J., and C. W. Harris, eds. 1966. *Analyses of concept learning* . . . For part of an edited book, it follows the title of the book, for example, *Analyses of concept learning*. Edited by H. J. Klausmeier and C. W. Harris . . . or Chap. 1 in *Analyses of concept learning*, edited by H. J. Klausmeier and C. W. Harris . . .

The title of a series follows the book title, for example, *North and South*. The Civil War Series . . .

In the above, notice that the words *edition* and *editor* are abbreviated the same way, (i.e., ed.).

Periodicals

Periodicals include journals, magazines, and newspapers. The parts of the reference to a journal article include the author's name, year, title of article, title of periodical, issue information, and page reference. The initials of the first author follow the surname; those of the second and later authors precede the surname. The titles of articles are capitalized as in sentences; subtitles may be omitted. The titles of periodicals are italicized and given regular title capitalization; the titles may be abbreviated. Arabic numerals are used for the volume number and the issue number, when applicable. The volume number and the issue number are not italicized.

Journal article, no author.

> Instructions in regard to preparation of a manuscript. 1929. *Psychological Bulletin* 26: 57-63.

Journal article, one author.

> Klausmeier, H. J. 1992. Concept learning and concept teaching. *Educational Psychologist* 27: 267-286.

Journal article, two authors.

Wilt, S., and S. Olson. 1996. Prevalence of domestic violence in the United States. *Journal of American Medical Women's Association* 51: 77-82.

Journal article, three authors.

Woodall, W. G., D. K. Davis, and H. Sahin. 1983. From the boob tube to the black box: Television news comprehension from an information processing perspective. *Journal of Broadcasting* 27: 1-23.

Journal article, more than three authors.

Deater-Deckard, K., S. Scarr, K. McCartney, and M. Eisenberg. 1994. Paternal separation anxiety: Relationships with parenting stress, child-rearing attitudes, and maternal anxieties. *Psychological Science* 5: 341-346.

Journal, issue number, month or season.

The issue number, when applicable, follows the volume number, for example, *American Psychologist* 54(4): 252-259.

The month or season, when applicable, follows the volume number, for example, *Social Security Bulletin* 28 (January): 3-29.

Magazine article.

Merkin, D. 1998. Freud rising. *New Yorker*, 9 November, 50-55.

Daily newspaper article, discontinuous pages.

Goode, E. 1998. New hope for losers in the battle to stay awake. *The New York Times*, 3 November, D1, D8.

Reviews in Periodicals

Review, book.

Klausmeier, H. J. 1968. Review of *Essentials of learning: An overview for students of education.* 2nd ed., by R. M. W. Travers. *Contemporary Psychology* 13:574.

Review, movie.

Kauffman, S. 1989. Turbulent lives. Review of *A dry white season* (MGM movie). *New Republic,* 9 October, 24-25.

Personal Communications

Underwood, Benton. 1982. Telephone conversation with the author, 13 April.

Feldhusen, John F. 1996. Letter to the author, 22 November.

Unpublished Material

Dissertations and theses.

Seltzer, M. 1990. The use of data augmentation in fitting hierarchical models to educational data. Ph.D. diss., University of Chicago.

Klausmeier, H. J. 1947. An experiment with two methods of teaching social studies in high school. Master's thesis, Indiana State University.

Rigney, J.C. 1962. A developmental study of cognitive equivalence transformations and their use in the acquisition and processing of information. Honors thesis, Radcliffe College.

Downright, A. B. 1993. Narrative diffusion and the professional editor. Ph.D. diss., University of Chicago, 1992. Abstract in *Dissertation Abstracts International* 52:3245A-3246A.

Papers and symposium contributions.

Klausmeier, H. J. 1977. Individual differences in cognitive development during the school years. Paper read at 85th Annual Convention of the American Psychological Association.

Klausmeier, H. J. 1985. Effects of schooling on students' educational development. Paper read at *XX* Interamerican Congress of Psychology at Caracas, Venezuela.

Klausmeier, H. J. 1979. Experience and cognitive development. Paper presented at symposium, International Symposium on Physics, Biology, and Mathematics: Different Approaches in an Integrated Curriculum for the Primary School, 24-28 January, at Italian Academy of Science, Rome.

Special Types of References

Widely used reference works, such as encyclopedias, and special works, including the Bible, plays, poems, and English, Greek, and Roman classics are generally not included in the reference list. Citations to these works are made in the text.

Public Documents

The reference list entry for a public document and the text citation should begin with the same element followed by the date. Additional information, examples of references, and the text citations for various kinds of public documents follow. The entries for the reference list, where applicable, come first, then the text citations in parentheses. (Some of the examples that follow and other examples may also be found in the 1993 *Chicago Manual of Style.*)

Hearings

> U. S. House, 1945. Committee on Banking and Currency. *Bretton Woods Agreements Act: Hearings on H. R.* 3314. 79th Cong., 1st sess.
>
> U. S. Senate, 1985. Committee on Foreign Relations. *Famine in Africa: Hearing Before the Committee on Foreign Relations.* 99th Cong., 1st sess. 17 January.

In-text citation

(House, 1945, 12-14)
(Senate, 1985, 53, 57)

Laws, Public Acts, and Statutes

Statutes are first published separately as slip laws. Slip laws, also referred to as public laws, are collected in the *United States Statutes at Large*, which is published annually. Subsequently the statutes are entered in the *United States Code*, revised every six years.

Slip laws are cited in the text. The citation of a slip law includes the following: its number, the session of Congress that enacted it, and the date it was approved.

Slip laws.

> U. S. Public Law 585. 79th Cong., 2d sess., 1 August 1946. *Atomic Energy Act of 1946.*
>   or
> *Atomic Energy Act of 1946.* U.S. Public Law 585. 79th Cong., 2d sess., 1 August 1946.

> In-text citation

> > (U. S. Public Law 585)
> >   or
> > (Atomic Energy Act of 1946)

Statutes cited in the *U.S. Statutes at Large.*

> U.S. Statutes at Large. 1947. Vol. 60, pp. 755-75. *Atomic Energy Act of 1946.*
>   or
> *Atomic Energy Act of 1946. U.S. Statutes at Large* 60:755-75.

> In-text citation

> > (Statutes at Large 1947, 767, 774)
> >   or
> > (Atomic Energy Act of 1946, 767, 744)

Statutes entered in the *U.S. Code.*

> *Declaratory Judgment Act.* 1952. *U.S. Code.* Vol. 28, secs. 2201-2.

> In-text citation

> > (*Declaratory Judgment Act of 1952*)

Executive Department Documents

Reports and bulletins are issued by executive departments, bureaus, and agencies. The citation in the text gives only the first element of the reference in the reference list, the date, and the pages.

> Treasury Department. Bureau of Prohibition. 1929. *Digest of Supreme Court decisions interpreting the National Prohibition Act and Willis-Campbell Act.* Washington, DC: GPO.

Straus, Ralph I. 1959. *Expanding private investment for free world economic growth.* A special report prepared at the request of the Department of State. April.

U.S. Bureau of the Census. 1975. *Median gross rent by counties of the United States, 1970.* Prepared by the Geography Division in cooperation with the Housing Division, Bureau of the Census. Washington, D.C.

Task force report: Juvenile delinquency and youth crime. 1967. President's Commission on Law Enforcement and Administration of Justice. Washington, DC: GPO.

In-text citation

(Treasury Department 1929, 14-28)
(Straus 1959, 12)
(U. S. Bureau of the Census 1975)
(*Task force report* 1967, 21)

Federal Court Decisions

References to federal court decisions are rarely given in the reference list. The date, the case, the court, and the location in the *United States Supreme Court Reports* (U.S.), *Supreme Court Reporter* (Sup. Ct.), or the Federal Court Reporter (F) are cited in the text as is indicated in the following examples:

In 1944, *Associated Press v. United States* (326 U. S. 1), the decision . . .
In 1990, *Maryland v. Craig* (110 Sup. Ct. 3157), the . . .
The United States Court of Appeals, Eighth Circuit, in *United States v. Rouse* (F.3d 360 [1966], found that . . .

International Bodies

In the reference list, publications of the League of Nations, the United Nations, and other international bodies include the name of the organization, the date, the topic or the title, the location of the organization, and identifying information for the topic or title. The text citation gives the name of the organization, the date, and pages when applicable.

League of Nations. 1944. *International currency experience: Lessons of the inter-war period.* Geneva. II.A.4.

United Nations. Secretariat. 1951. Department of Economic Affairs. *Methods of financing economic development in underdeveloped countries.* II.B.2.

UNESCO. 1963. *The development of higher education in Africa.* Paris.

In-text citation

(League of Nations 1944)
(UN Secretariat 1951)
(UNESCO 1963, 145)

Nonbook Materials

Nonbook materials include sound recordings, slides and films, and video-cassettes. In the reference list, the entry for a sound recording (e.g., music, lecture) includes the writer, composer, or other person followed by the date, the title of the work, and the director or other person, if applicable. The title of the work is italicized. The recording company and the number of the recording or other identifying information may be added. An indication of the kind of recording (e.g., audiocassette) is entered at the close of the reference if the information is not part of the title.

The style for nonbook references in the reference list allows more flexibility for writers than does the style for books and journal articles. However, consistent use throughout a manuscript is required. The style for text citations is the same as that for authors and anonymous works.

Mozart, Wolfgang Amadeus. *Symphony no. 38 in D major.* Vienna Philharmonic. James Levine. Polydor compact disk 423 086-2.

Klausmeier, H. J. 1991. *Concept learning and concept teaching.* Audiotape of paper presented at meeting of the American Psychological Association, San Francisco, August 1991. Washington, DC: American Psychological Association.

Moral development and Individually Guided Education. 1977. 16 mm, 17 min. Reading, MA: Addison-Wesley. Filmstrip.

The unit leader in Individually Guided Education. 1977. 16 mm, 25 min. Reading, MA: Addison-Wesley. Film.

Sylvester, R. 1998. *On social interaction and brain development.* 40 min. 1998 Bloomington, IN: Phi Delta Kappa. Videocassette.

In-text citation

(Mozart. Symphony no. 38 in D major. Vienna Philharmonic. Levine)
(Klausmeier 1991)
(Moral development and Individually Guided Education 1977)
(The unit leader in Individually Guided Education 1977)
(Sylvester 1998)

Computer Software and Electronic Documents

Computer Software

Computer software includes programs, languages, systems, and the like. In the reference list, the entry gives the title, except for widely known items (e.g., COBOL, FORTRAN); identifying details (e.g., version, level, release number, or date); the short name or acronym, where applicable, enclosed in parentheses; and the location and name of the supplier. The author's name may be mentioned if it aids identification.

The software is cited in the text. The citation typically includes all of the preceding information except the location and the name of the supplier.

FORTRAN H-extended Version [*or* Ver.] 2.3. IBM, White Plains, NY.

Lotus 1-2-3 Rel. 2. Lotus Development Corporation, Cambridge, MA.

Operating System/Virtual Storage Rel. 1.7 (OS/VS 1.7). IBM, White Plains, NY.

Statistical Package for the Social Sciences Level M Ver. 8 (SPSS Lev. M 8.1). SPSS, Chicago.

In-text citation

FORTRAN H-extended Version [or Ver.] 2.3
Lotus 1-2-3 Rel. 2
Operating System/Virtual Storage Rel. 1.7 (OS/VS 1.7)
Statistical Package for the Social Sciences Level M Ver. 8 (SPSS Lev. M 8.1)

Electronic Documents

The International Standards Organization (ISO) has developed a uniform system for citing electronic material and continues to update it. The U.S. office branch of ISO is:

> American National Standards
> 1142 West 42nd Street
> New York, NY 10036

The document that updates *The Chicago Manual of Style* (1993) is *Excerpts From International Standard 690-2: Information and Documentation–Bibliographic References–Part 2: Electronic Documents or Parts Thereof* (American National Standards, 1997). The Web address for this document retrieved August 25, 2000) from the World Wide Web is:

> http://www.nlc-bnc.ca/iso/tc46sc9/standard/690-2e.htm

Citations of electronic documents are beginning to appear in some journals. Journal editors can inform manuscript authors whether a journal follows the 1993 style or the 1997 update.

Sample Reference List

In the reference list, the entries are listed alphabetically. A one-author work precedes a multiauthor work that begins with the same surname as the one-author work. Works by the same author(s) are listed by the year of publication, the earliest year first. Works by the same author(s) with the same year of publication are arranged by the title of the works, excluding A or The; lowercase letters–a, b, c, and so on–are placed immediately after the year. Works having a group author or no authors are entered by the first significant word in the name, except that the full names of official groups are given.

Exhibit A1 shows implementation of the preceding guides. The list includes different kinds of authorship and various works that typically appear in the reference lists of research journal articles.

The references in Exhibit A1 are identical to those in Exhibit 7.2, except that those in Exhibit 7.2 conform to the style given in the 1994 *Publication Manual of the American Psychological Association.*

**Exhibit A1. Sample Reference List That Conforms to the
1993 *Chicago Manual of Style***

American Association of University Women. 1992. *How schools short change girls: The AAUW report.* New York: Marlowe.

Clarke-Stewart, K. A., C. P. Gruber, and L. M. Fitzgerald. 1994. *Children at home and in day care.* Hillsdale, NJ: Erlbaum.

Downright, A. B. 1993. Narrative diffusion and the professional editor. Ph.D. diss., University of Chicago, 1992. Abstract in *Dissertation Abstracts International* 52:3245A-3246A.

Fredrick, W. C., and H. J. Klausmeier. 1968a. Concept identification as a function of the number of relevant and irrelevant dimensions, presentation method, and salience. *Psychological Reports* 23: 631-634.

_____. 1968b. Instructions and labels in a concept-attainment task. Psychological Reports 23:1339-1342.

Goode, E. 1998. New hope for losers in the battle to stay awake. *The New York Times,* 3 November, D1, 8.

Klausmeier, H. J. 1968. Review of *Essentials of learning: An overview for students of education.* 2nd ed., by R. M. W. Travers. *Contemporary Psychology* 13:574.

_____. 1977. Individual differences in cognitive development during the school years. Paper read at 85th Annual Convention of the American Psychological Association.

_____. 1979. Experience and cognitive development. Paper presented at symposium, International Symposium on Physics, Biology, and Mathematics: Different Approaches in an Integrated Curriculum for the Primary School, 24-28 January, Rome, Italian Academy of Science.

_____. 1985. Personality integration and classroom discipline. Chap. 13 in *Educational psychology,* 5th ed. New York: Harper & Row.

_____. 1991. *Concept learning and concept teaching.* Audiotape of paper presented at meeting of the American Psychological Association, San Francisco, August, 1991. Washington, DC: American Psychological Association.

_____. 1992. Concept learning and concept teaching. *Educational Psychologist* 27:267-286.

_____. 1996. The role of the researcher in educational improvement: A retrospective analysis. Chap. 5 in *Intellectual Talent: Psychometric and Social Issues,* edited by C. B. Benbow and D. Lubinski. Baltimore, MD: The Johns Hopkins University Press.

Klausmeier, H. J., and P. S. Allen. 1978. *Cognitive development of children and youth: A longitudinal study.* New York: Academic Press.

Klausmeier, H. J., and C. W. Harris, eds. 1966. *Analyses of concept learning.* New York: Academic Press.

Merkin, D. 1998. Freud rising. *New Yorker,* 9 November, 50-55.

Morris, J. A., ed. 1997. *Practicing psychology in rural areas: Hospital privileges and collaborative care.* Washington, DC: American Psychological Association.

Piaget, J. 1971. *Psychology and epistemology: Towards a theory of knowledge.* Translated by A. S. Rosin. New York: Viking Press.

Sandoval, J., C. Frisby, K. Geisinger, J. Ramos-Grenier, and J. Scheuneman, eds. 1998. *Test interpretation and diversity: Achieving equity in assessment.* Washington, DC: American Psychological Association.

Seltzer, M. 1990. The use of data augmentation in fitting hierarchical models to educational data. Ph.D. diss., University of Chicago.

Woodall, W. G., D. K. Davis, and H. Sahin. 1983. From the boob tube to the black box: Television news comprehension from an information processing perspective. *Journal of Broadcasting* 27:1-23.

APPENDIX B. JOURNALS IN PSYCHOLOGY AND IN EDUCATION GROUPED ACCORDING TO CONTENT AND REJECTION RATES

The sole purpose of this Appendix is to show the large differences in the rejection rates of journals that publish the same kind of subject matter. Lists of journals in two subfields of psychology are given, arranged in groups from highest to lowest rejection rates. There is a similar list of education journals. All of the journals devote half or more of their content to research stud ies–empirical, review, or theoretical. There are many other journals that cover the same content as the journals in these three groups.

The rejection rates are given in 10-point intervals; however, the two original publications that follow give a precise percentage for each journal. The intervals are used here inasmuch as some variation in the rate occurs across the years.

Journals in Psychology: A Resource Listing for Authors (American Psychological Association, 1997) provides much more information about the listed journals and many others in psychology and related fields. Henson (1999) gives more information on education journals.

General

90% or higher
  Canadian Psychology
  Journal of Humanistic Psychology
  Journal of Polymorphous Perversity
80-89%
  American Psychologist
  Journal of Mind and Behavior
  Psychological Methods
  Teaching of Psychology
70-79%
  Behavior and Philosophy

British Journal of Psychology
European Psychologist
Evolution and Human
  Behavior
Humanistic Psychologist
International Journal of
  Psychology
Psychological Bulletin
Theory and Psychology
World Psychology

(Continued)

60-69%
The American Journal of
Psychology
Journal of the History of the
Behavioral Sciences
Journal of Theoretical and
Philosophical Psychology
Psychological Reports
Psychological Review
Psychology: A Journal of Human
Behavior

50-59%
Genetic, Social, and General
Psychology Monographs
Journal of Psychohistory
40-49%
Journals of Psychology:
Interdisciplinary and Applied
Psychological Record
39% or lower
Irish Journal of Psychology
Journal of General Psychology

Treatment

90% or higher
Journal of Sex Research
Psychology of Women Quarterly
80-89%
British Journal of Psychotherapy
Behavioral Medicine
Journal of Marriage and the Family
Journal of Pediatric Psychology
Women & Therapy
70-79%
Behavior Therapy
Contemporary Psychoanalysis
Family Process
Family Relations
Journal of Child Psychology and
Psychotherapy
Journal of Clinical Child Psychology
Journal of Family Psychology
60-69%
Counseling Psychologist
Family Therapy
Infant Mental Health Journal
Journal of Clinical Psychoanalysis
Journal of Youth and Adolescence

50-59%
Behavior Modification
Behavioural and Cognitive
Psychotherapy Education and
Treatment of Children
Journal of Cognitive Psycho-
therapy
Journal of Family Psycho-
therapy
Journal of Family Therapy
Journal of Homosexuality
Journal of Sex Education and
Therapy
Sexual and Marital Therapy
40-49%
Developmental
Neuropsychology
International Forum for
Logotherapy: Journal of
Search for Meaning

Educational Research in Education Journals

90% or higher
  American Educational Research Journal
  Harvard Educational Review
  Phi Delta Kappan
  Planning and Changing
  Teachers College Record
80-89%
  Clearing House
  Comparative Education Review
  Journal of Experimental Education
  Merrill-Palmer Quarterly
  Review of Educational Research
70-79%
  American Journal on Mental Retardation
  Learning and Individual Differences
  Professional Educator
60-69%
  Creative Child and Adult Quarterly
50-59%
  Education and Treatment of Children
  Educational Assessment
39% or lower
  Journal of Instructional Psychology

APPENDIX C. MANUSCRIPT SUBMISSION LETTER, EDITORS' EVALUATIONS OF SUBMITTED MANUSCRIPTS, AND EVALUATION FORMS FOR MANUSCRIPT REVIEWERS

In this Appendix, the template of a manuscript submission letter was prepared by the *Handbook* author. For the other materials supplied by colleagues, the letterheads, author signatures, and logos and addresses identifying a university or journal have been deleted to save space. The format of the material has been changed to be consistent with that of the *Handbook*. However, the content has not been changed in any way. For their important contributions I am deeply appreciative and thank the following:

Editor's evaluation of a manuscript accepted conditional on revision for *Parenting for High Potential*–**Donald J. Treffinger, Editor**.

Editor's evaluation of a manuscript accepted conditional on revision for the *Review of Educational Research* and a Manuscript Evaluation Form for reviewers of manuscripts submitted to the *Review of Educational Research*–**Elizabeth Graue, Professor,** Department of Curriculum and Instruction, University of Wisconsin, Madison, **Associate Editor**.

Reviewer's Check List for reviewers of manuscripts submitted to *Environment and Behavior*–**Robert B. Bechtel, Professor,** Department of Psychology, University of Arizona, **Editor**. (This journal has a relatively low rejection rate. Note that the Check List calls for reviewers to give suggestions for improving a manuscript.)

Template of a Manuscript Submission Letter Prepared in Accord with the Style Recommended in the Publication Manual of APA

Date

Journal editor's name and address

Salutation:

Enclosed are \<number\> copies of a manuscript entitled \<manuscript title\>. The length of the manuscript is \<number\> pages, and there are \<number\> tables and figures. \<Provide the editor general information, for example, whether the manuscript is based on a dissertation, whether the research has been reported at a scientific meeting, or whether a closely related manuscript has been published or submitted for publication\>. Please consider the manuscript for publication in \<name of journal\>.

Please direct correspondence to \<name of manuscript author, address, and email address\>. I look forward to hearing from you.

Sincerely,

\<Author's name and signature\>

Editor's Evaluation of a Manuscript Accepted
Conditional on Revision

Date

Manuscript author's name and address

Salutation:

I am pleased to inform you of our conditional acceptance of your manuscript, [insert number and title], for publication in a future issue of *Parenting for High Potential* Magazine. All manuscripts go through a very extensive review and evaluation process. Please read the following enclosures with this letter very carefully and promptly:

- **A summary of the feedback for your manuscript (if you have not already received this information via email from the editor).** The feedback describes the revisions and changes that will be necessary for you to make. With these changes, we will accept the manuscript without the need for further review. *It is extremely important that you respond to these recommendations as soon as possible, in order to avoid delays in scheduling.*

- **The author's release form.** Two copies of our standard release form are enclosed. Please sign and date them, and return one copy with your final manuscript. The other copy is for your files.

- **An instruction sheet for your response.** This sheet provides information about the procedures and time line for returning the final manuscript to us. Please follow these instructions carefully and promptly. Failure to do so may result in an extended delay in publishing your article!

Thank you for your valuable and interesting contribution to *Parenting for High Potential.* We will look forward to receiving your revised manuscript.

Cordially,

Donald J. Treffinger, Editor

Editor's Evaluation of a Manuscript Accepted
Conditional on Revision

Date

Manuscript author's name and address

Salutation:

We have recently received three reviews from scholars with expertise in the area addressed by your manuscript "Single-Sex and Coeducational Schooling: Relationships to Socioemotional and Academic Development" (Ms#067.97). The reviewers were generally quite favorable about this piece and supported its continued development for publication in the *Review of Educational Research*. They provided very complete feedback which should give you good direction as you rethink this paper. We would like to invite you to revise the work with their comments as a guide.

Methodological issues: Reviewer C noted that you address methodological issues at the end of the paper but that it is such a pervasive issue that it should be woven throughout your discussion. How does the framing of a study shape what we can know about the topic? How is this literature pointing toward a particular way of knowing and what are the gaps in our knowledge which could be addressed by other kinds of inquiry? How have we missed discussion of within-gender differences?

Evenhandedness: Reviewer A was uneasy about the arguments put forward and against coeducational and single-sex education. It would make sense to read carefully for balance.

Apples and oranges: It would be important to distinguish between single-sex schools and single-sex classrooms in this work.

Please read the reviewers' comments carefully as they have done some careful thinking about this manuscript. Given the positive responses you have received, we anticipate that, if you can make the requested revisions and provide us with a clear accounting of the revisions, we would not need to send it out for review again.

Please let us know how you would like to proceed with this manuscript. If you choose to revise the manuscript, please inform us as to when we can expect to receive the revised manuscript. With the revision, include a letter detailing how you have addressed the reviewers' concerns. The revised manuscript should run from 25 to 50 double-spaced, typewritten pages, and should be accompanied by an abstract of 100 to 150 words. Submit three hard copies and one diskette copy (in WordPerfect, IBM-compatible format) of the revised manuscript. We have kept the copies of your manuscript as a record for our files and to support any additional correspondence we may have.

Thank you for considering *RER* and we wish you success in your work.

Sincerely,
Carl A. Grant, Editor   Elizabeth Graue, Associate Editor
Joy L. Lei, Editorial Assistant

Manuscript Evaluation Form

Reviewer: _____

REVIEW OF EDUCATIONAL RESEARCH
Manuscript Evaluation Form

Date: _____

Manuscript #: _____

Reviewer #: _____

Please circle the appropriate rating for each standard for RER articles.

Criteria for *RER* articles:

	Low		Medium		High	
1. Quality of the literature reviewed	1	2	3	4	5	6
2. Quality of analysis	1	2	3	4	5	6
3. Significance of the topic reviewed	1	2	3	4	5	6
4. Impact of the review for						
a. educational practice	1	2	3	4	5	6
b. educational research	1	2	3	4	5	6
5. Degree to which the article advances the field	1	2	3	4	5	6
6. Degree to which the article is the appropriate length for its message and argument	1	2	3	4	5	6
7. Degree to which the article is well-written	1	2	3	4	5	6
8. Degree to which the review is balanced and fair	1	2	3	4	5	6

Editorial Recommendation: (check one)

1. Accept _____
2. Accept with minor revisions _____
3. Revise and re-submit _____
4. Reject
   a. Not consistent with *RER* standard _____
   b. Inappropriate for *RER* _____

Justification for the Recommendation:

On the reverse side of this sheet of paper or on a separate sheet of paper, please give your reasons for your editorial recommendation. Please be complete (addressing the above criteria) and formulate your reasons in a style that can be sent directly and anonymously to the author(s).

Please mark on the line if you would like to receive a copy of all the reviews for this manuscript. ____ .

(on reverse side)
REVIEW OF EDUCATIONAL RESEARCH
Comments for the author of Manuscript # _____
Reviewer # _____

Reviewer's Check List and Reviewer's Comments for the Journal: **Environment and Behavior**

TITLE OF PAPER:

Please fill out the following in addition to typed comments:

1. *Style:* Is the writing clear and unambiguous?
      Yes _____ No _____

If no, please give guidance for rewriting in your comments.

2. Theory: Is the connection with theory clearly made?
      Yes _____ No _____

If no, please suggest how this might be done?

3. Literature: Does the writer mention the necessary references?
      Yes _____ No _____

If no, please list the omitted ones in your comments.

4. Methods: Has the author used the proper methods?
      Yes _____ No _____

If no, please suggest more proper ones, or correct misuses.

5. Interpretation: Has the author given the appropriate interpretation to data?
      Yes _____ No _____

If no, please suggest better or alternative ones.

6. Significance: Is the paper a significant contribution to the field?
      Yes _____ No _____

If no, state reasons why.

7. *Final Judgment:*
_____ Should be published, top priority. No revision necessary.
_____ Should be published. No revision necessary.
_____ Should be published with revision.
_____ Should not be published.

(on reverse side)
Reviewer's Comments

TITLE OF PAPER:

Please type. Do not sign.

Do you object to sending a copy to the author? Yes_____ No_____

If you feel the paper should not be published as it now stands, please state what changes might be made to make it publishable (refer to the check list).

APPENDIX D. FORMATS FOR ELECTRONIC REFERENCES RECOMMENDED BY THE AMERICAN PSYCHOLOGICAL ASSOCIATION (1999, NOVEMBER 19)

ELECTRONIC REFERENCE FORMATS RECOMMENDED BY THE AMERICAN PSYCHOLOGICAL ASSOCIATION*

- Citing Email Communications
- Citing a Web Site
- Citing Specific Documents on a Web Site
- Citing Articles and Abstracts From Electronic Databases
- Web Citations in Text

Citing Email Communications

First, a cautionary note: It is possible to send an email note disguised as someone else. Authors—not journal editors or copy editors—are responsible for the accuracy of all references, which includes verifying the source of mail communications before citing them as personal communications in manuscripts.

Email communications from individuals should be cited as personal communications, as noted in APA's *Publication Manual* (4th ed., pp. 173-174). The format in text (personal communications are not cited in the reference list) is as follows: L. A. Chafez (personal communication, March 28, 1997).

Citing a Web Site

To cite an entire Web site (but not a specific document on the site), it's sufficient to give the address of the site in the text. For example,

---

*© 1999 American Psychological Association (Reprinted with permission).
Last update: November 19, 1999
Note: This document replaces "How to Cite Information From the Internet and the World Wide Web."

Kidspsych is a wonderful interactive Web site for children (http://www.kidspsych.org).

No reference entry is needed.

Citing Specific Documents on a Web Site

Web documents share many of the same elements found in a print document (e.g., authors, titles, dates). Therefore, the citation for a Web document often follows a format similar to that for print, with some information omitted and some added. Here are some examples of how to cite documents posted on APA's own Web site.[1]

An action alert posted by our Public Policy Office:

> American Psychological Association. (1995, September 15). *APA public policy action alert: Legislation would affect grant recipients* [Announcement]. Washington, DC: Author. Retrieved January 25, 1996 from the World Wide Web: http://www.apa.org/ppo/ istook.html

An article from the journal *American Psychologist*:

> Jacobson, J. W., Mulick, J. A., & Schwartz, A. A. (1995). A history of facilitated communication: Science, pseudoscience, and antiscience: Science working group on facilitated communication. *American Psychologist, 50*, 750-765. Retrieved January 25, 1996 from the World Wide Web: http://www.apa.org/journals/jacobson.html

An article from the *APA Monitor* (a newspaper):

> Sleek, S. (1996, January). Psychologists build a culture of peace. *APA Monitor*, pp. 1, 33. Retrieved January 25, 1996 from the World Wide Web: http://www.apa.org/monitor/peacea.html

An abstract:

> Rosenthal, R. (1995). *State of New Jersey v. Margaret Kelly Michaels: An overview [Abstract]*. Psychology, Public Policy, and Law, 1, 247-271. Retrieved January 25, 1996 from the World Wide Web: http://www.apa.org/journals/ab1.html

This document:

> *Electronic reference formats recommended by the American Psychological Association.* (1999, November 19). Washington, DC: American Psychological Association. Retrieved November 19, 1999 from the World Wide Web: http://www.apa.org/journals/webref.html

All references begin with the same information that would be provided for a printed source (or as much of that information as is available). The Web information is then placed in a retrieval statement at the end of the reference. It is important to give the date of retrieval because documents on the Web may change in content, move, or be removed from a site altogether. In fact, none of the examples above are currently available on APA's Web site.

Citing Articles and Abstracts From Electronic Databases

APA's recommendations for citing electronic media have changed substantially since we published the fourth edition of the *Publication Manual.* For databases, rather than the "Available: File: Item:" statement specified in the *Publication Manual,* we now recommend a retrieval statement that identifies the date of retrieval (omitted for CD-ROMs) and the source (e.g., DIALOG, WESTLAW, SIRS, Electric Library), followed in parentheses by the name of the specific database used and any additional information needed to retrieve a particular item. For Web sources, a URL should be given that points to an "entry page" for the database. The basic retrieval statement for CD-ROM databases is as follows:

> Retrieved from [source] database ([name of database], CD-ROM, [release date], [item no.–if applicable])

The basic retrieval statement for on-line databases is:

> Retrieved [month day, year] from [source] on-line database ([name of database], [item no.–if applicable])

The basic retrieval statement for databases accessed via the Web is:

> Retrieved [month day, year] from [source] database ([name of database], [item no.–if applicable]) on the World Wide Web: [URL]

Examples:

Federal Bureau of Investigation. (1998, March). *Encryption: Impact on law enforcement.* Washington, DC: Author. Retrieved from SIRS database (SIRS Government Reporter, CD-ROM, Fall 1998 release)

Schneiderman, R. A. (1997). Librarians can make sense of the Net. *San Antonio Business Journal, 11*(31), pp. 58+. Retrieved January 27, 1999 from EBSCO database (Masterfile) on the World Wide Web: http://www.ebsco.com

Kerrigan, D. C., Todd, M. K., & Riley, P. O. (1998). Knee osteoarthritis and high-heeled shoes. *The Lancet, 251,* 1399-1401. Retrieved January 27, 1999 from DIALOG database (#457, The Lancet) on the World Wide Web: http://www.dialogweb.com

Davis, T. (1992). Examining educational malpractice jurisprudence: Should a cause of action be created for student-athletes? *Denver University Law Journal, 69,* 57+. Retrieved [month day, year] from WESTLAW on-line database (69 DENULR 57)

Bowles, M. D. (1998). The organization man goes to college: AT&T's experiment in humanistic education, 1953-1960. *The Historian, 61,* 15+. Retrieved [month day, year] from DIALOG on-line database (#88, IAC Business A.R.T.S., Item 04993186)

Web Citations in Text

Follow the author/date format described on pages 168-174 in the *Publication Manual.* To cite specific parts of a Web document, indicate the chapter, figure, table, or equation as appropriate.

For quotations, give page numbers (or paragraph numbers) if they are available. If page or paragraph numbers are not available (i.e., they are not visible to every reader), they can be omitted from the in-text citation. With most browsers, readers will still be able to search for the quoted material.

---

[1]In new browsers (4.0 and higher), the citation examples will appearing in "hanging-indent" style (i.e., the first line is flush left and all subsequent lines are indented). In older browsers, the citation examples will appear in block format. (This is not APA style, but rather a limitation of paragraph display in older browsers.) For papers or manuscripts, either a regular paragraph indent or a hanging indent is appropriate for references, as long as the format is consistent throughout. For additional information on acceptable paragraph formatting for references, see our *Publication Manual FAQ.*

In addition, italics are used in place of underlining. As with the paragraph indent, either italics or underlining is acceptable in an APA-style manuscript, providing they are used consistently.

Finally, the examples are single spaced rather than double-spaced. This is also a browser limitation–APA style calls for references to be double spaced.

INDEX

A

Abbreviated manuscript, 12
Abbreviations
  abbreviation of
    academic degrees, 47
    acronyms, 41
    chemical compounds, concentrations, 51
    initials for names, 51
    Latin terms enclosed in parentheses, 50
    legal references, 78, 93ñ94
    names of tests, 50
    nonlegal references, 78
    states and territories, 51
    statistical terms table, 57
    technical terms, 50
    units of measurement, 50, 51
    United States, 51
  forming plurals of, 51
    in statistical and mathematical material, 56-58
    misuses of, 51
    uses with abstracts and statistical terms, 51
    using periods with, 51
Abstract (*See also* References in the reference list)
  abbreviations in, 99
  citations in, 99
  conciseness of, 12
  in reference list
    original source, 83
    secondary source, 83
  key words in, 98
  length of, for
    empirical study, 99
    review of article, 99
  numbers in, 99
  on CD-ROM, 91
  self-contained, 98
  spacing, 98
  writing an, 98-99
Abstract terms, 19 (*See also* Writing style)

Adjectives, 26-27
Adverbs, 26-27
Aging, avoiding language bias, 35-36
  care needing versus care providing, 35
  individual differences among older people, 35
  research on, 35
  stereotyping language, vi, 6
Alphabetizing in reference list, 94
American Educational Research Association
  mentoring for research publication, ix
American Psychological Association
  mentoring for research publication, ix
American Psychological Association style
  (*See also Publication Manual of the APA*)
  APA Style Helper 2.0, viii
  Electronic Formats Recommended by the APA, viii (*see also* Appendix D)
  Publication Manual of the APA, vi-viii, 6, 10, 11, 31, 37, 56
Analysis of completed work, 13-14, 18-21
Appendix A, *Chicago Manual of Style*
  reference citations, 108-25
  Index, 112-25
  sample reference list, 126-27
  table of contents, 108-11
Appendix B, journals and rejection rates, 128-30
Appendix C, manuscript submission, 131-37
  editor's evaluation, conditional acceptance, 133
  editor's evaluation, revision conditions, 134-35
  manuscript evaluation form, 136-37
  submission letter, APA style, 132
Appendix D, electronic references formats, 138-42
  in reference list
    abstract, 139
    action alert, 139
    article
      journal, 139

newspaper, 139
CD-ROM database, 140
document, 140
email communications, 138
website
  database, 140-41
  documents, 139-40
reference citations in text
web documents, 141-42
APA Monitor, viii, 3
Apostrophe, 44-45
in contractions, 45
in possessive form of nouns and pronouns, 44, 45
to form plurals, 45
Arabic numerals, 52
ASCII file, 98
Assistance, expert
academic sources, viii, 5-6, 102
confidential consultation sources, viii, 102
peer review, 5, 102
professional organizations, ix, 102
Asterisks, 68
Author
acknowledgment of contributions, 4
affiliation of, 98
byline, example of, 98
certification of, 100
example of author note, 66
name, 4, 98
responsibilities, 104
Author note, 65-66
example of, 66
information provided in, 65-66
submitting, 66
typing, 65
Authors in reference citations in text
anonymous, 75
groups as, 75
multiple
  six or more, 74
  three, four, or five, 74
  two, 74
  two or more with same surname, 75
no author, 75
of parts of a source, 76
one, 73
two or more publications in same
  parentheses, 76

Authorship
agreement on, 4
certification of, 4
manuscript based on a dissertation, 4, 12-14
order of authors, 4
responsibilities, 4
Avoiding Heterosexual Bias in Language, 30

B
Benefits from getting research published
access to ideas worldwide, 3
advancing in position, 3
advancing knowledge, 3
feelings of successful achievement, 3, 7
obtaining desired position, 3
publish or perish, 3
raise in salary, 3
satisfaction, 3
Bias in language
aging, vi, 6, 35-36
disabilities, vi, 6, 33-34
gender, vi, 6, 34-35
race and ethnicity, vi, 6, 32-33
sexual orientation, vi, 6, 31-32
Book chapters
in reference list, 85, 86
Book review
in reference list, 89
Booklet
in reference list, 84
Books (*See also* Appendix A, *Chicago Manual of Style*)
in reference list
  dictionary, 83
  dictionary on CD-ROM, vii, 91
  English translation, 84
  encyclopedia, 85
  group author, government agency, 84
  private agency, 84
  no author or editor, 83
  non-English, 84
  one author, 83
  one editor, 85
  republished, 84
  six or more authors, 84
  three to five authors, 83
  three to five editors, 85
  two authors, 83

two editors, 85
Brackets
  in quotations, 42
  in mathematical material, 42
  with commas, 42
  with parentheses, 42
Brief Report, 14

C

Camera-ready manuscript, 10, 100
Capitalization
  capitalize
    abbreviations of academic degrees, 47
    first word after colon, 46
    first word of heading, 47
    main words in titles, 46
    name of experimental condition or
      group, 47
    nouns followed by numeral or letter, 46
    proper nouns, 46
    titles of tests, 47
Captions for figures, 71
Cassette recording
  in reference list
    music, 89
    speaker, 89
    video, 90
Certification of authorship, 4
CD-ROM
  in reference list
    abstract of doctoral dissertation on, 90, 91
    dictionary on, vii, 91
Charts, 69, 70
Chicago Manual of Style, vi, vii, ix, 6, 37, 56,
  111-27
  Appendix A
    examples of conformity to style, 126-27
  Index to reference citations, 111-25
  Table of Contents, 108-10
Colon
  between place of publication and
    publisher's name, 38
  in ratios and proportions, 38
  preceding
    clarifying material, 38
    list or summary, 38
    quotation, 38
Comma
  in citing references, 40

in giving exact dates, 40
in numbers, 55
in series, 39
misuses, 40
nonrestrictive clauses, 39
with dependent and independent clauses,
  39, 40
Computer software (*See also* Appendix D)
  in reference list, 92
Conciseness
  and sentence development, 13-14
Concrete terms
  and sentence development, 19-20
Conjunctions, 28-29
  coordinating, 28
  correlative, 29
  subordinating, 29
Content footnotes, 65, 66
Converting dissertation into an article, 12-14
Copies of manuscript
  for submission, 10-11, 100
Copyediting, 103
Copy editor, 103
Court decisions (*See also* Appendix A)
  cases
    citing in text, 93-94
    in reference list, 93-94
Cover letter to editor, 82 (*See also* Appendix
  C)
Criteria for evaluating study, v, 5

D

Dangling modifier, 25-26
Dash, 40
*Dictionary of Bias-Free Usage: Guide to
  Nondiscriminatory Language,* 31
Dictionaries, vii, 91
Disabilities, avoiding language bias, vi, 6, 33-
  34
  barriers, definitions, 33
  expressions with negative connotations, 34
  handicapping mental and physical barriers,
    33
  impairment, 33
  labels for, 34
Dissertation
  converting to manuscript, 12-14
  in reference list, 90
Doctoral candidates

and evaluation of empirical study, 5, 14
converting dissertation to manuscript, 12-14
review of dissertation, ix, 4-6, 12-14
Drawings, 70

E
Editorial style, definition of, 37
Electronic Reference Formats Recommended by the American Psychological Association, viii, 91-92 (*See also* Appendix D)
Electronic media
in reference list, 91-92 (*see also* References in reference list)
Electronic Style: Guide for Citing Electronic Information (1993), 92
Electronic Styles: Handbook for Citing Electronic Information (1996), 92
Elements of Style, vii, viii
Ellipsis points
to indicate omission of material, 45
with quotations, 45
Empirical study
criteria for evaluating quality of, v, 5
organization of headings, 12
Et al., 74
Ethnicity and race, avoiding language bias, 32-33
capitalization, 33
Ethics in manuscript writing
authorship, 4
acknowledgement protocol, 4
dissertation chairperson, 4
correction after publication, 4, 104
credits, 4
data storage, 4, 103
honesty and reliability, 3
original publication, 4
nonfabricated data, 4
permissions, 4
Evaluating quality of empirical study
hypotheses, 5
literature review, 5
participants, 5
procedure, 5
reliability and validity of data gathering devices, 5
research design, 5
research question, 5

results, 5
statistical analyses, 5
Executive order, 94
Expert assistance
evaluation of study, 5
dissertation committee, 6
experienced researcher, 5
peer review, 5
in writing manuscript, viii-ix
with editorial review of manuscript, viii-ix, 5-6
Expository style (*See also* Writing style)
competence in conforming to style, 6-7, 15-36
definition, 15
effective sentences, 6-7,
logical sequence of ideas, 15-16
unified paragraphs, 16-18
word choice, 18-21

F
Failure, motive to avoid, 3, 7
manuscript submission, v, 3, 7
Figures
captions and legends, 71
charts, 69, 70
flow, 70
organizational, 70
schematics, 70
citing in text, 71
deciding to use, 69
drawings, 69, 70
figures versus text, 69
glossy prints, 72
graphs, 69
bar, 69
circle, 69
line, 69
scatter, 69
general guides for, 69
handling, 72
kinds of, 69
numbering, 72
photographs, 69, 71
black-and-white, 71
color, 71
cropping, 71
permission to reproduce, 71
quantitative information in, 69

reduction and enlargement of, 71
size and proportion of, 71
submitting, 72
versus tables, 69
Film
in reference list, 90
Footnotes
content, 65, 66
numbering, 66
permission, 65, 66
submitting, 66

G

Gender, avoiding language bias, vi, 6, 34-35
APA policy regarding, 34
sexist language, 34-35
terms related to, 34-35
Grammar
adjectives and adverbs, 26-27
conventional use of, 26
misplacing, 27
since, 27
verb phrases as, 26
while, 27
conjunctions, 28-29
coordinating, 28
correlative, 29
subordinating, 29
nouns, 22
parallel construction, 29-30
elements within sentences, 30
ideas among sentences, 29
items of a series, 29
names of men and women, 30
prepositions and prepositional phrases, 27-28
choice of prepositions, 27
prepositional phrase, misplacement of, 28
words followed by specific prepositions, 28
pronouns, 22-23
agreement of
indefinite pronouns and nouns, 22, 23
personal pronoun and gender, 23
nominative and objective case of, 22
none, 23
possessive case of indefinite pronouns, 23

possessive case preceding present
participle, 23
that and *which*, 22
their and *his/her*, 23
verbal phrases, 24-26
gerund, 24
infinitive, 24
participle, 24
verbs, 24-26
active voice, 24
agreement in number, 24, 25
with noun closer to verb, 25
with subject, 25
dangling and or misplaced modifier, 25-26
retention of verb in clauses, 25
subjunctive mood, 26
verbs versus nouns, 24
use of, 24
Graphs, 69
Guidelines for Avoiding Racial/Ethnic Bias in Language, 30
Guidelines for Nonhandicapping Language in APA Journals, 30
Guidelines for Nonsexist Language in APA Journals, 30

H

Handbook, overview of chapter contents, v-ix
Headings in manuscripts
levels of, 59-62
style protocols, 59
manuscript with
four levels of, 62
three levels of, 61
two levels of, 60
Hyphenation
hyphenate
compound constructions, 48
prefixes of base words, 48
"selfi" words, 48
misuses, 49

I

Importance of getting first manuscript
published, 7
Indefinite pronoun agreement, 23
Italics

italicize by underlining
    letters in statistical terms, 49, 58, 98
    letters, words, and phrases used as
        examples, 49, 98
    scale and test scores, 49, 98
    technical terms, 49, 98
    titles of books and periodicals, 49, 98
    words that could be misread, 49, 98
    material not italicized, 49, 50

J
Journal articles (*See also* References in
    reference list)
    conversion of dissertation into article, 12-14
        empirical, 10, 14
        review, 10
        theoretical, 10
Journal selection
    acceptance rate for manuscripts, v, 6, 9 (*see
        also* Appendix B)
    author instructions, 10, 11
    editor, contact for information, 12
    kinds of articles published
        empirical studies, 6
        reviews, 6
    manuscript requirements, 9-12
        American Educational Research Journal, 10
        Journal of Educational Psychology, 11
        *Journals in Psychology: Resource Listing for
            Authors,* 9
        Psychological Abstracts, 10
    research subject matter, 9, 11
    review procedures, 6, 9-12
    selection guidelines, 9-12
Journals (*See also* References in reference list;
    Appendix A)
    charges and page allocation, 6
    in reference list (*see also* journal articles)
        published annually, 82
        special issue, 82
    rejection rates, 6
    selection guidelines, 9-12
*Journals in Psychology: A Resource Listing for
    Authors,* 9 (*See also* Appendix B)

K
Kinds of manuscripts
    empirical study, 10
    review of literature, 10

theoretical, 10

L
Legal material
    citing and in reference list
        court decisions, 93-94
        executive order, 94
        legislative material, 93
        statutes, 93
Location of publishers
    major cities, 77

M
Magazine articles (*See also* Appendix A)
    in reference list, 81
Manuscript (*See also* Writing style)
    abbreviated, 12
    abstract, 98-99
    after publication of
        making corrections, 4, 103
        retaining data, 4, 103
    author responsibilities for, 4, 97, 104
    based on dissertation, 12-14
    benefits from publishing, 3
    bias in language, avoiding, vi, 6, 30-36
    developing plan for writing, 8-14
    expository style, 6-7, 15-36
    grammar, usage, 6
    in reference list, 90, 91
    italics indicated by underlining, 49, 58, 98
    journal selection/submission guidelines, 9-
        12 (*see also* Appendix C)
        editor
            conditional acceptance, 100-1
            contact for information, 12
            cover letter, 100
            review comparable articles, 11
    levels of headings in, 12
    number of copies, 11, 12, 100
    obstacles that impede writing, 7-12 (*see also*
        Obstacles that impede manuscript
        writing)
    preparing and submitting, 97-100
        abstract, 98-99
        copies, 11, 12, 100
    cover letter, 100 (*see also* Appendix C)
        certification of authorship, 4
        general information, 100
        specific information, 100

verification of meeting ethical
standards, v, 3-4, 11
order of pages, 99
accompanying material, 99
text, 99
title page, 98
page numbering and page headers, 99
page specifications, 97-98
word processing specifications, 97-98
reference citations and reference lists
editorial style
conforming to *Chicago Manual of Style*,
vi, vii, 10, 37 (*see also* Appendix A)
conforming to *Publication Manual of
APA*, vi-ix, 6, 10, 11, 31, 37, 56, 97
electronic formats, 91-92 (*see also*
Appendix D)
general, vi, 73-96
responding to editorial review
manuscript
abstract, 98-99
accepted conditional on revision, 100-
1 (*see also* Appendix C)
expert assistance, securing, 5-6, 102
rejected, 101-2
rejected with encouragement for
revision, 102 (*see also* Appendix C)
review and proofreading, 102-3
copyedited manuscript, 103
typeset proof, 103
title page, preparation of, 98
word processing, 97-98
writing style, vi, 15-36 (*see also* Writing
style)
sequencing, logical order, 15-16
unified paragraphs, 16-18
Manuscript submission
brevity and conciseness, 13-14
central problem focus, 13
literature review brevity, 13
methodology essentials, 13
selective presentation of results, 14
state problem concisely, 13
cover letter, 100 (*see also* Appendix C)
editorial evaluation, conditional
acceptance, 100-1 (*see also* Appendix C)
evaluation form (*see* Appendix C)
information sources
American Educational Research Journal, 10

Journal of Educational Psychology, 11
*Journals in Psychology: Resource Listing for
Authors*, 9
Psychological Abstracts, 10
preparation of multiple formats, 12
review of literature, 12
summary and highlights, 12
theory clarification, 12
Mathematical material, 56-59
abbreviations and symbols, 56
frequently used, 56, 57
mathematical equations, 59
table of, 57
analysis of variance, 58
chi-square, 58
correlation, 58
descriptive statistics, 58
Greek, 56, 57
parameters, 56
writing out, 56
parentheses, 42
path analysis, 58
population statistics, 56
regression analysis, 58
text rather than symbol, 58
Merriam-Webster's Collegiate Dictionary, vii, 47,
103
proofreader mark translations, 103
Meta-analysis references in reference list, 77
Metric measurement, 55-56
for metric measures and conversion tables
see
*American National Standard for Metric
Practice*
Chicago Manual of Style
Merriam-Webster's Collegiate Dictionary
Publication Manual of APA
Misplaced modifier, 25-26
Monographs
in reference list
bound into a journal, 82
with issue and serial number, 82
Methodology
manuscript presentation, 13

N
New Oxford Guide to Writing, vii
Newsletter articles
in reference list

no author, 81
one author, 81
Newspaper articles (*See also* Appendix A)
  in reference list
  daily, 81
  letter to editor, 82
  monthly, 82
Notes (*See also* Footnotes)
  author note, 65-66
    example of, 66
    information provided in, 65-66
    submitting, 66
    typing, 65
  table notes, 68
    general, 68
    probability, 68
    specific, 68
Noun strings
  avoidance of, 21
Nouns, 22
Numbers
  combining figures and words to express
    back-to-back modifiers, 55
    rounded large numbers, 55
  commas in and not in, 55
    groups of three digits, 55
  expressed in figures
    age, 53
    dates, 53
    fractional and decimal quantities, 54
    mathematical functions, 54
    numbered series, 53
    numbers in lists, 53
    participants, 53
    part of book or table, 53
    percentiles, 54
    ratios, 54
    samples and populations, 53
    scores, 53
    specific place in numbered series, 53
    sums of money, 53
    ten (10) and higher, 53
    time, 53
  expressed in words
    beginning of heading, title, or sentence, 54
    below 10, 53
    common fractions, 54
    widely accepted terms, 54

forming plurals of, 55
ordinal numbers, 55

O

Obstacles that impede manuscript preparation
  evaluating journal requirements as too difficult, 9-12
    lacking information about journal rejection rates, 6
    motive to avoid failure, 7
    not having suitable environment for writing, 8-9
    not setting aside time for writing, 8
    overestimating competence required, 7
    underestimating significance of own study, 7
On-line sources (*See also* Appendix D)
  in reference list, 91-92
Oral presentation of study
  informal, viii
  paper at a meeting, viii
  poster session, viii
  symposium, viii
Ordinal numbers, 55
Outline for manuscript, 12 (*See also* Planning to write)

P

Paper presentations
  in reference list
    at conferences, 88
    at international meetings, 88
    at national meetings, 88
    lectures, 87
Paragraph development, 16-18 (*See also* Writing style)
Parallel construction, 29-30
Parentheses
  enclosing letters in a series, 41
  enclosing page numbers of quotation, 41
    (*see also* Quotations)
  enclosing peripheral material, 41
  in introducing abbreviations, 41
  in reference citations, 41
  with other punctuation, 41-42
Period
  misuses with abbreviations, 51
  use with

abbreviations, 47, 50, 51
  academic degrees, 47
    Latin terms, 50
  ellipsis points, 45
  parentheses, 41
  quotation marks, 44
Personal communications, 76
Permission footnotes, 65, 66
Photographs, 71
Planning to write a manuscript, 8-14
  based on dissertation, 12-14
  ethical considerations, v, 3-4, 11
  journal editor, contact for information, 12
    (*see also* Appendix C)
  journal selection, 9-12 (*see also* Appendix B)
    review comparable articles, 11
  manuscript length requirements, 12-14
  manuscript, multiple presentations, 12
  physical environment, 8-9
  preparing outline, 12
  time schedule, 8
Preparing outline for manuscript, 12
  empirical study organization headings, 12
Prepositions and prepositional phrases, 27-28
  choice of prepositions, 27
  prepositional phrase, misplacement of, 28
  words followed by specific prepositions, 28
Presenting Your Findings: Practical Guide for Creating Tables, 67
Pronouns, 22-23
  agreement of
    indefinite pronouns and nouns, 22, 23
    personal pronoun and gender, 23
  nominative and objective case of, 22
  none, 23
  possessive case of indefinite pronouns, 23
  possessive case preceding present
    participle, 23
  that and *which*, 22
  their and *his/her*, 23
Proofreader's marks, 103
PsycINFO, 10
Psychological Abstracts, viii, 10
Publication charges, 6
Publication Manual of the APA, vi-ix, 6, 10, 11, 31, 37, 56
Punctuation
  apostrophe, 44-45
  brackets, 42

colon, 38
comma, 39-40, 43
dash, 40
ellipsis points, 43, 45
parentheses, 41-42
period, 37, 44
question mark, 37, 43
quotation marks, 43-44, 63
semicolon, 38-39, 43
slash, 45

Q

Quality of empirical study
  hypotheses, 5
  literature review, 5, 11, 12
  organization of headings, 12, 59
  participants, 5
  procedure, 5
  reliability and validity of data gathering
    devices, 5
  research design, 5
  research question, 5
  results, 5
  statistical analyses, 5
Question mark, 37
Quotation marks (double)
  incorrect uses, 44
  set off instructions to participants, 43
  set off test item, 43
  set off title of article or chapter, 43
  with other punctuation, 43
Quotations
  adding emphasis to, 44, 63
  block, 63
  crediting sources and securing permission,
    64
    500-word rule, 64
  direct, 63
  entering in manuscript, 63
  entering page number of, 63
  indirect, 63
  italics, use of, 63
  length
    fewer than 40 words, 63
    more than 40 words, 64
  omitting part of material, 45
  punctuation
    ellipsis points, 45
    parentheses, 41

quotation marks, 43
reproducing quoted material, 63
set off instruction, 43
set off title, 43
misuses, 44

R
Race and ethnicity, avoiding language bias,
  vi, 6, 30, 32-33
  negative comparison of groups, 33
  precise specification of study participants,
    32-33
  preferred name of group, 32
  terms eliciting biased conclusions, 33
Redundancy, avoidance of, 19
Reference citations in the text (*See* Appendix
  A for *Chicago Manual of Style*)
  accuracy of, 73
  agreement with reference list, 73
  anonymous work, 75
  groups as authors, 75
  no author, 75
  one author, 75
  parts of a source, 76
  personal communications, 76
  six or more authors, 74
  three, four, or five authors, 74
  two authors, 74
  two authors with same surname, 75
  two or more publications enclosed in
    parentheses by
    different authors, 76
    same authors and same publication date,
      76
    same authors in different years, 76
Reference lists (*See also* Appendix A)
  for *Handbook*, 105-7
  example conforming to
    APA style, 95-96
    Chicago Manual of Style, 126-27 (*see also*
      Appendix A)
    electronic formats, 91-92 (*See also*
      Appendix D)
References in reference list (*See also*
  Appendix A)
  abbreviation of terms in
    legal references, 78, 93-94
    nonlegal references, 78
    states and territories, 77, 79

abstracts
  original source, 83
  secondary source, 83
accuracy and completeness of, 73
alphabetizing names, 94
authors (*see* journal articles)
APA style for, 95-96
audiovisual media
  cassette recording
    music, 89
    speaker, 89
    video, 90
  film, 90
  television
    broadcast, 90
    series, 90
    single episode in series, 90
book articles and chapters
  group author, one editor, 86
  in encyclopedia, 85
  one author, two editors, 85
  two authors, series and volume editors,
    86
  two authors, two editors, 86
book supplement, 85
booklet, 84
books (*see* Books)
computer software, 92
court decisions, 92
doctoral dissertations
  abstracted, 90
  unpublished, 90
editors
  one, 85
  three to five, 85
  two, 85
electronic media (*see also* Appendix D)
  CD-ROM, abstract of doctoral
    dissertation, 91
  CD-ROM, dictionary, 91
  computer software, 91-92
  on-line abstract, 91
  on-line database, 91-92
  on-line journal article, general access, 91
  on-line journal article, subscriber based,
    91
executive order, 94
general, 73-94
journal articles

in press, 81
no author, 80
non-English, translated, 80
on-line, 92
one author, 80
reply to other authors, 81
six or more authors, 80
supplement, 81
three, four, or five authors, 80
two authors, 80
legislative material, 93
location of publishers, 77
magazine articles
  Jr. in author's name, 81
  one author, 81
manual, 84
manuscripts
  submitted for publication, 9-12, 88
  unpublished, 88
monographs
  bound into journal, 82
  with issue and serial number, 82
newsletter articles
  no author, 81
  one author, 81
newspaper articles
  daily, 81
    discontinuous pages, 82
    no author, 81
  monthly, 82
    letter to editor, 82
    one author, 82
paper presentations
  at conferences, 88
  at international meetings, 88
  at national meetings, 88
  lectures, 87
research and technical reports available
  from
  Educational Resource Information
    Center, 86
  Government Printing Office, 86
  National Technical Information Service,
    86
  private source, 87
  technical report from university, 87
  U.S. government agency, not GPO, 87
  university, 87
  working paper from university, 87

reviews
  book, 89
  film, 89
statutes, 93
symposium contributions
  published in edited book, 88
  published in symposium proceedings, 88
tests, published
  achievement, 89
  intelligence, 89
theses, unpublished
  honors, 91
  master's, 91
  working paper,
Reference selection, 77
Rejection of manuscript
  main cause, 9
  journal, selection of appropriate, 9 (*see also*
    Journal selection)
    acceptance rate, 9
    editor, contact for information, 12
    research subject matter, 9
    review of comparable articles, 11, 12
    selection guidelines, 9
Rejection rates of journals, vi, 6 (*See also*
  Appendix B)
Research and technical reports
  in reference list, 86-87
Research results
  presentation for manuscript publication, 14
Responding to editorial review, 100-2
Review and proofreading, 102-3
  copyedited manuscript, 103
  typeset proof, 103
Review of literature, 11, 12
Roget's International Thesaurus, vii

S
Semicolon
  after a closing parenthesis, 39
  after conjunctive adverbs, 39
  between independent clauses, 38, 39
  between series that contain commas, 39
  outside closing quotation marks, 39
Sentence development, 15-36 (*See also*
  Writing style)
  sentence development, 18-22
    abstract versus concrete terms, 19-20
    brief, 18, 19

concise, vi, 18
grammar, rules of, vi, 22-36 (*See also* Grammar)
length requirements, 12-14
logical, 21
noun strings, avoidance of, 21
precise meanings, 20-21
punctuation to show relationships, 21
redundancy, avoidance of, 19
referents of simple pronouns, 20
sentence length, 19
word choice, 18-21
   abstract versus concrete, 19-20
   precise meaning, 20
   wordiness, avoidance of, 18
unified paragraph development, 16-21
  transitional words
   faulty use of, 16-18
   logical relationships and, 16, 21
   omission of, 16-17
  verbs, needless switching
   subject of, 18
   tense of, 17
   voice of, 17
Seriation
  capitalizing first word after colon, 52
  marking items of series with
   Arabic numerals, 52
   lowercase letters, 52
  use of
   comma in series, 52
   semicolon in series, 52
Sexual orientation, avoiding language bias, vi, 6, 31-32
  bisexual, 31
  demeaning terms, 32
  gay men, 31
  heterosexual, 31
  homosexual, 31
  lesbian, 31
  sexual behavior references, 31-32
  sexual preference versus sexual orientation, 31
   incorrect usage of term, 31
  stereotypic terms, 31
Significance of research study, 101-2
Since, 27
Slash
  faulty use of, 45

  with common fractions, 45
Spelling, 47
  Consult *Merriam-Webster's Collegiate Dictionary* or *Webster's Third New International Dictionary*. Use preferred choice when more than one is given.
Statistical and mathematical material
  abbreviations and symbols, 56
   frequently used, 56, 57
   mathematical equations, 59
   table of, 57
  analysis of variance, 58
  chi-square, 58
  correlation, 58
  descriptive statistics, 58
  Greek, 56, 57
  parameters, 56
   writing out, 56
  parentheses, 42
  path analysis, 58
  population statistics, 56
  regression analysis, 58
  text rather than symbol, 58
Statutes
  citing in text, 93
  in reference list, 93
Submission of footnotes, 66
Submission of manuscript (*See also* Appendix C)
  order of other material, 99
  order of pages of text, 99
Symposium contributions
  in reference list
   published in edited book, 88
   published in symposium proceedings, 88

T
Tables
  citing in text, 68
  explaining in text, 68
  headings
   abbreviations in, 67
   symbols in, 67
  locating examples of, 67
  notes
   asterisks in, 68
   general, 68
   ordering, 68
   placement of, 68

probability, 68
  specific, 68
  superscripts in, 68
numbering, 68
ruling, 67
  horizontal, 67
  length, 67-68
submitting, 68
title of, 67
versus text presentation, 67
Table notes, 68
Table rules
  horizontal, 67
  length, 67-68
Tense of verb
  avoid unnecessary switching of, 17
Tests, published
  in reference lists
    achievement, 89
    intelligence, 89
That, 22
Their, 23
Theoretical study, 10
Theses, unpublished
  in reference list
    honors, 91
    master's, 91
Typeface
  bold, 56
  italic, 56, 98
  standard, 56
Typing
  abbreviations
    Latin terms, 50
    legal terms, 78
    nonlegal terms, 78
    states and territories, 79
    statistical symbols, 57
    technical terms, 50
    units of measurement, 50-51
  abstract, 98-99
  author byline, 98
  author note, 65-66
  author's institutional affiliation, 98
  capitalization, 46-47
  care in, 97
  double-spacing, 97-98
  ellipsis points, 45, 64
  figure captions and legends, 71-72
  footnotes, 65-66

headings, 99
hyphenation, 48-49
indention and no indention, 98
italics, 49, 58, 98
lines per page, 98
manuscript header, 99
margins
  no justification, 98
  one-inch, 98
note, author, 65-66
number of copies, 100
numbers on pages, 99
0 and 1 versus letters O and l, 97
page and text order, 99
paper, 97
pica or elite type size, 97
punctuation, 37-45, 51
reference list, 73-96, 111-25
running head, 98
seriation, 52
special characters, use of, 97
title page, 98
typeface, 56, 97
underlining rather than italicizing, 49, 58, 98
uppercase and lowercase letters, 98

U
Underlining, 49, 58, 98

V
Verb phrases, 24
Verbs, 24-26
  active voice, 24
    agreement in number, 24, 25
      with noun closer to verb, 25
      with subject, 25
    dangling and or misplaced modifier, 25-26
    retention of verb in clauses, 25
    subjunctive mood, 26
    verbs versus nouns, 24
    use of, 24
Verification of meeting ethical standards, v, 3-4, 11

W
Web (*See* World Wide Web)
Webster's Dictionary (*See Merriam-Webster's Collegiate Dictionary*)
Which, 22

While, 27
World Wide Web (www)
  electronic media, 91-92 (*see also* Appendix
  D)
Wordiness, avoidance of, 18
Word choice, 18-21
Word Into Type, vii
Word processing (*See also* Typing)
  abbreviations
    Latin terms, 50
    legal terms, 78
    nonlegal terms, 78
    states and territories, 79
    statistical symbols, 57
    technical terms, 50
    units of measurement, 50-51
  abstract, 98-99
  author byline, 98
  author note, 65-66
  author's institutional affiliation, 98
  capitalization, 46-47
  care in, 97
  double-spacing, 97-98
  ellipsis points, 45, 64
  figure captions and legends, 71-72
  footnotes, 65-66
  headings, 99
  hyphenation, 48-49
  indention and no indention, 98
  italics, 49, 58, 98
  lines per page, 98
  manuscript, 97-98
  manuscript header, 99
  margins
    no justification, 98
    one-inch, 98
  note, author, 65-66
  number of copies, 100
  numbers on pages, 99
  0 and 1 versus letters O and l, 97
  page and text order, 99
  paper, 97
  pica or elite type size, 97
  punctuation, 37-45, 51
  reference list, 73-96, 111-25
  running head, 98
  seriation, 52
  special characters, use of, 97

title page, 98
typeface, 56, 97
underlining rather than italicizing, 49, 58,
  98
uppercase and lowercase letters, 98
unformatted ASCII file, 98
Words
  choice of, 18-21
  combined with figures to express numbers,
    55
  numbers expressed in, 54
Write Right, vii
Writing style
  expository style, definition, 15
  logical sequence of manuscript parts, 15-16
    discussion and implications, 12
  expository style competence, 6-7, 15-36
    introduction, heading term, 12
    method, 12
    results, 12
  review of journal articles, 11, 12
  sentence development, 18-22
    abstract versus concrete terms, 19-20
    brief, 18, 19
    concise, vi, 18
    grammar, rules of, vi, 22-36
    length requirements, 12-14
    logical, 21
    noun strings, avoidance of, 21
    precise meanings, 20-21
    punctuation to show relationships, 21
    redundancy, avoidance of, 19
    referents of simple pronouns, 20
    sentence length, 19
    word choice, 18-21
      abstract versus concrete, 19-20
      precise meaning, 20
    wordiness, avoidance of, 18
  unified paragraph development, 16-21
    transitional words
      faulty use of, 16-18
      logical relationships and, 16, 21
      omission of, 16-17
    verbs, needless switching
      subject of, 18
      tense of, 17
      voice of, 17

Appendix A: Table of Contents re *Chicago Manual of Style*, 108-11

Appendix A: Index re *Chicago Manual of Style*, 112-25
Abbreviations of words in reference
  citations in text for
    appendix, 112
    figure, 112
    note, 112
    page(s), 112
Additional works by same author
  in reference citations in text, 113
Author
  in reference citations in text, 111-12
Basic form of reference citations in text, 111-13 (*See also* Reference citations)
Books
  in reference list
    anonymous work, 115
    basic form of reference citation, 114
    chapters, 116
    editions, 117
    editors, 115, 117
    foreword to, 116
    groups as author, 114
    in process of publication, 15
    more than three authors, 115
    more than three editors, 115
    multivolumes, 117
    non-English, 115
    one author, 114
    one editor, 115
    parts of book, 116
    series, 117
    three authors, 114
    translated, 115
    two authors, 114
    two editors, 115
Computer software
  in reference list, 124
Dissertations and theses
  in reference list, 119
Electronic documents
  in reference list, 125
International bodies
  in reference list
    League of Nations, 122
    UNESCO, 123
    United Nations, 123

Nonbook materials
  in reference list
    film, 123
    filmstrip, 123
    recording, 123
    videocassette, 123
Papers and symposium contributions
  in reference list, 119
Parts of a book
  authors of also authors of book, 116
  chapter
    author of also author of book, 116
    one author, two editors, 116
Periodicals
  basic form of reference citation, 117
  in reference list
    daily newspaper article, 118
    journal
      issue number, 118
      month or season, 118
    journal article
      more than three authors, 118
      no author, 117
      one author, 117
      three authors, 118
      two authors, 118
    magazine article, 118
    review in periodicals
      book, 118
      movie, 119
Personal communications
  in reference list, 119
Public documents
  in reference list
    executive departments, 121-22
    federal court decisions, 122
    hearings, 120
    laws, public acts, statutes, 121-22
Reference citations in text
  additional works by same author
    with pages given, 113
    without pages given, 113
  appendix, abbreviation for, 112
  author rather than work, 111
  books, parts of, 116
  computer software, 124
  electronic documents, 125
  executive department documents, 122
  federal court decisions, 122
  figure, abbreviation for, 112

government agency as author, 112
groups as author, 112
hearings, Congress, 120
international bodies, 123
more than three authors, 112
  more than three authors, another work of
    same date, 112
nonbook materials, 124
note, abbreviation for, 112
one author, 111
page(s), abbreviation for, 112
slip laws, 121
statutes, 121
three ways to enter citations
  author and date enclosed in parentheses,
    113
  author other than self, date enclosed in
    parentheses, 113
  self as author, date not enclosed in paren
    theses, 113
two different authors
  same last name, same date, 111
two family members
  same last name, 111
two or more sources
  in one parenthetical citation, 113
two or three authors, 111
volume and page number
  more than one volume, 113
  one volume, 113
References in the reference list
  books (*see* Books)
  computer software,124
  electronic documents, 125
  international bodies
    League of Nations, 122
    UNESCO, 123
    United Nations, 123
  nonbook materials
    film, 123
    filmstrip, 123
    sound recordings
      music, 123
      speaker, 123
    videocassette, 123
  periodicals, 117

personal communications, 119
public documents
basic form of reference citation, 120
  hearings,120
  executive departments, 121-22
  federal court decisions, 122
  slip laws, 121
  statutes
    cited in *U.S. Statues at Large*, 121
    entered in *U.S. Code*, 121
special types of
  reference works, 120
  special works, 120
unpublished material
  dissertations and theses, 119
  papers and symposium contributions, 119
Volume and page numbers
  in reference citations, 117

**Appendix B: journals in psychology and
education and rejection rates**, 128-30

Appendix C: manuscript submission,
131-37
  editor's evaluation, conditional acceptance,
    133
  editor's evaluation, revisions, 134-35
  manuscript evaluation form, 136-37
  submission letter, APA style, 132

**Appendix D: electronic references for-
mats**, 138-42
  in reference list
    abstract, 139
    action alert, 139
    article
      journal, 139
      newspaper, 139
    CD-ROM database, 140
    document, 140
    email communications, 138
    web site(s)
      database, 140-41
      documents, 139-40
  reference citations in text
    web documents, 141-42